The Book *of* Job

WITH A PREFACE BY

Cynthia Ozick

VINTAGE SPIRITUAL CLASSICS

VINTAGE BOOKS
A DIVISION OF RANDOM HOUSE, INC.
NEW YORK

A VINTAGE SPIRITUAL CLASSICS ORIGINAL, DECEMBER 1998

FIRST EDITION

Library of Congress Cataloging-in-Publication Data
Bible. O.T. Job. English. Revised Standard. 1998.
The Book of Job / with a preface by Cynthia Ozick. — 1st ed.
p.   cm. — (Vintage spiritual classics)
ISBN 0-375-70022-6 (alk. paper)
1. Bible. O.T. Job—Commentaries.   I. Title.   II. Series.
BS1413199 8
223'.1077—dc21   98-11792
CIP

www.randomhouse.com

Book design by Fritz Metsch

Printed in the United States of America.
10 9 8 7 6 5 4 3 2 1

CONTENTS

by John F. Thornton and Susan B. Varenne, General Editors

A turn or shift of sorts is becoming evident in the reflections of men and women today on their life experiences. Not quite as adamantly secular and, perhaps, a little less insistent on material satisfactions, the reading public has recently developed a certain attraction to testimonies that human life is leavened by a Presence that blesses and sanctifies. Recovery, whether from addictions or personal traumas, illness, or even painful misalignments in human affairs, is evolving from the standard therapeutic goal of enhanced self-esteem. Many now seek a deeper healing that embraces the whole person, including the soul. Contemporary books provide accounts of the invisible assistance of angels. The laying on of hands in prayer has made an appearance at the hospital bedside. Guides for the spiritually perplexed have risen to the top of best-seller lists. The darkest shadows of skepticism and unbelief, which have eclipsed the presence of the Divine in our rational age, are beginning to lighten and part.

If the power and presence of God are real and effective, what do they mean for human experience? What does He offer to men and women, and what does He ask in return? How do we recognize Him? Know Him? Respond to Him? God has a reputation for being both benevolent and wrathful. Which will He be for me and when? Can these aspects of the Divine somehow be reconciled? Where is God when I suffer? Can I lose Him? Is God truthful, and are His promises to be trusted?

Are we really as precious to God as we are to ourselves and our loved ones? Do His providence and amazing grace guide our faltering steps toward Him, even in spite of ourselves? Will God abandon us if the sin is serious enough, or if we have episodes of resistance and forgetfulness? These are fundamental questions any person might address to God during a lifetime. They are pressing and difficult, often becoming wounds in the soul of the person who yearns for the power and courage of hope, especially in stressful times.

The Vintage Spiritual Classics present the testimony of writers across the centuries who have considered all these difficulties and who have pondered the mysterious ways, unfathomable mercies, and deep consolations afforded by God to those who call upon Him from out of the depths of their lives. These writers, then, are our companions, even our champions, in a common effort to discern the meaning of God in personal experience. For God is personal to us. To whom does He speak if not to us, provided we have the desire to hear Him deep within our hearts?

Each volume opens with a specially commissioned essay by a well-known contemporary writer that offers the reader an appreciation of its intrinsic value. For the Book of Job, commentaries by some of its most insightful readers have also been provided.

We offer a final word about the act of reading these spiritual classics. From the very earliest accounts of monastic practice—dating back to the fourth century—it is evident that a form of reading called *lectio divina* ("divine" or "spiritual reading") was essential to any deliberate spiritual life. This kind of reading is quite different from that of scanning a text for useful facts and bits of information, or advancing along an exciting plot line to a climax in the action. It is, rather, a meditative approach, by which the reader seeks to taste and savor the beauty and truth of every phrase and passage. This process of contemplative reading has the effect of enkindling in the reader compunction for past behavior that has been less than beautiful and true. At the same time, it increases the desire to seek a realm where all that is lovely and unspoiled may be found. There are four steps in *lectio divina:* first to read, next to meditate, then to rest in the sense of God's nearness, and, ultimately, to resolve to govern one's actions in the light of new understanding. This kind of reading is itself an act of prayer. And, indeed, it is in prayer that God manifests His Presence to us.

by Cynthia Ozick

The riddles of God are more satisfying than the solutions of men.
—G. K. CHESTERTON

What the Scholars Say

Twenty-five centuries ago (or perhaps twenty-four or twenty-three), an unnamed Hebrew poet took up an old folktale and transformed it into a sacred hymn so sublime—and yet so shocking to conventional religion—that it agitates and exalts us even now. Scholars may place the Book of Job in the age of the Babylonian Exile, following the conquest of Jerusalem by Nebuchadnezzar—but to readers of our own time, or of any time, the historicity of this timeless poem hardly matters. It is timeless because its author intended it so; it is timeless the way Lear on the heath is timeless (and Lear may owe much to Job). Job is a man who belongs to no known nation; despite his peerless Hebrew speech, he is plainly not a Hebrew. His religious customs are unfamiliar, yet he is no pagan: he addresses the One God of monotheism. Because he is unidentified by period or place, nothing in his situation is foreign or obsolete; his story cannot blunder into anachronism or archaism. Like almost no other primordial poem the West has inherited, the Book of Job is conceived under the aspect of the universal—if the universal is understood to be a questioning so organic to our nature that no creed or philosophy can elude it.

That is why the striking discoveries of scholars—whether through philological evidences or through the detection of infusions from surrounding ancient cultures—will not deeply unsettle the common reader. We are driven—we common readers—to approach Job's story with tremulous palms held upward and unladen. Not for us the burden of historical linguistics, or the torrent of clerical commentary that sweeps through the centuries, or the dusty overlay of partisan interpretation. Such a refusal of context, historical and theological, is least of all the work of willed ignorance; if we choose to turn from received instruction, it is rather because of an intrinsic knowledge—the terror, in fact, of self-knowledge. Who among us has not been tempted to ask Job's questions? Which of us has not doubted God's justice? What human creature ever lived in the absence of suffering? If we, ordinary clay that we are, are not equal to Job in the wild intelligence of his cries, or in the unintelligible wilderness of his anguish, we are, all the same, privy to his conundrums.

Yet what captivates the scholars may also captivate us. A faithful English translation, for instance, names God as "God," "the Lord," "the Holy One," "the Almighty"—terms reverential, familiar, and nearly interchangeable in their capacity to evoke an ultimate Presence. But the author of Job, while aiming for the same effect of incalculable awe, has another resonance in mind as well: the dim tolling of some indefinable aboriginal chime, a suggestion of immeasurable antiquity. To achieve this, he is altogether sparing in his inclusion of the Tetragrammaton, the unvocalized YHVH (the root of which is "to be," rendered as "I am that I am"), which chiefly delineates God in the Hebrew Bible. Instead, he sprinkles his poem, cannily and profusely, with pre-Israelite God names—El, Eloah, Shaddai—names so lost in the long-ago, so unembedded in usage, that the poem is inevitably swept clean of traditional pieties. Translation veils the presence— and the intent—of these old names; and the necessary seamlessness of translation will perforce paper over the multitude of words and passages that are obscure in the original, subject to philological guesswork. Here English allows the common reader to remain untroubled by scholarly puzzles and tangles.

But how arresting to learn that Satan appears in the story of Job not as that demonic figure of later traditions whom we meet in our translation but as *ha-Satan,* with the definite article attached, meaning "the Adversary"—the counterarguer among the angels, who is himself one of "the sons of God." Satan's arrival in the tale helps date its composition. It is under Persian influence that he turns up—via Zoroastrian duality, which pits, as equal contenders, a supernatural power for Good against a supernatural power for Evil. In the Book of Job, the scholars tell us, Satan enters Scripture for the first time as a distinct personality and as an emblem of destructive forces. But note: when the tale moves out of the prose of its fablelike frame into the sovereign grandeur of its poetry, Satan evaporates; the poet, an uncompromising monotheist, recognizes no alternative to the Creator, and no opposing might. Nor does the poet acknowledge any concept of afterlife, though Pharisaic thought in the period of his writing is just beginning to introduce that idea into normative faith.

There is much more that textual scholarship discloses in its search for the Job-poet's historical surround: for example, the abundance of words and phrases in Aramaic, a northwestern Semitic tongue closely related to Hebrew, which was rapidly becoming the lingua franca of the post-Exilic Levant. Aramaic is significantly present in other biblical books as well: in the later Psalms, in Ecclesiastes, Esther, and Chronicles—and, notably, in the Dead Sea Scrolls. The Babylonian Talmud is written in Aramaic; it is the language that Jesus speaks. Possibly the Job-poet's everyday speech is Aramaic—this may account for his many Aramaisms—but clearly, for the literary heightening of poetry, he is drawn to the spare beauty and noble diction of classical Hebrew (much as Milton, say, in constructing his poems of Paradise, invokes the cadences of classical Latin).

And beyond the question of language, the scholars lead us to still another enchanted garden of context and allusion: the flowering, all over the ancient Near East, of a form known as wisdom literature. A kind of folk philosophy linking virtue to prudence, and pragmatically geared to the individual's worldly success, its aim is instruction in levelheaded judgment and in the achievement of rational contentment. The biblical Proverbs belong to this genre, and, in a more profoundly reflective mode, Ecclesiastes and portions of Job; but wisdom literature can also be found in Egyptian, Babylonian, Ugaritic, and Hellenistic sources. It has no overriding national roots and deals with personal rather than collective conduct, and with a commonsensical morality guided by principles of resourcefulness and discretion. A great part of the Book of Job finds its ancestry in the region's pervasive wisdom literature (and its descendants in today's self-improvement bestsellers). But what genuinely seize the heart are those revolutionary passages in Job that violently contradict what all the world, yesterday and today, takes for ordinary wisdom.

What the Reader Sees

However seductive they are in their insight and learning, all these scholarly excavations need not determine or deter our own reading. We, after all, have in our hands neither the Hebrew original nor a linguistic concordance. What we do have—and it is electrifying enough—is the Book of Job as we readers of English encounter it. And if we are excluded from the sound and texture of an elevated poetry in a tongue not ours, we are also shielded from problems of structure and chronology, and from a confrontation with certain endemic philological riddles. There is riddle enough remaining—a riddle that is, besides, an elemental quest, the appeal for an answer to humankind's primal inquiry.

So there is something to be said for novice readers who come to Job's demands and plaints unaccoutred: we will perceive God's world exactly as Job himself perceives it. Or put it that Job's bewilderment will be ours, and our kinship to his travail fully unveiled, only if we are willing to absent ourselves from the accretion of centuries of metaphysics, exegesis, theological polemics. Of the classical Jewish and Christian theologians (Saadia Gaon, Rashi, Ibn Ezra, Maimonides, Gersonides, Gregory, Aquinas, Calvin), each wrote from a viewpoint dictated by his particular religious perspective. But for us to be as (philosophically) naked as Job will mean to be naked of bias, dogma, tradition. It will mean to imagine Job solely as he is set forth by his own words in his own story.

His story, because it is mostly dialogue, reads as a kind of drama. There is no proscenium; there is no scenery. But there is the dazzling spiral of words—extraordinary words, Shakespearean words; and there are the six players, who alternately cajole, console, contradict, contend, satirize, fulminate, remonstrate, accuse, deny, trumpet, succumb. Sometimes we are reminded of *Antigone,* sometimes of *Oedipus* (Greek plays that are contemporaneous with Job), sometimes of *Othello.* The subject is innocence and power; virtue and injustice; the Creator and his Creation; or what philosophy has long designated as theodicy, the Problem of Evil. And the more we throw off sectarian sophistries—the more we attend humbly to the drama as it plays itself out—the more

clearly we will see Job as he emerges from the venerable thicket of
theodicy into the heat of our own urgency. Or call it our daily
breath.

Job's Story

Job's story—his fate, his sentence—begins in heaven, with Satan
as prosecuting attorney. Job, Satan presses, must be put to trial.
Look at him: a man of high estate, an aristocrat, robust in his
prime, the father of sons and daughters, respected, affluent, con-
scientious, charitable, virtuous, God-fearing. God-fearing? How
effortless to be always praising God when you are living in such
ease! Look at him: how he worries about his lucky children and
their feasting, days at a time—was there too much wine, did they
slide into blasphemy? On their account he brings sacred offerings
in propitiation. His possessions are lordly, but he succors the poor
and turns no one away; his hand is lavish. Yet look at him—how
easy to be righteous when you are carefree and rich! Strip him of
his wealth, wipe out his family, afflict him with disease, and *then*
see what becomes of his virtue and his piety!

So God is persuaded to test Job. Invasion, fire, tornado, destruction, and the cruelest loss of all: the death of his children.
Nothing is left. Odious lesions creep over every patch of Job's
skin. Tormented, he sits in the embers of what was once his
domain and scratches himself with a bit of shattered bowl. His
wife despairs: after all this, he still declines to curse God! She
means for him to dismiss God as worthless to his life, and to dismiss his ruined life as worthless. But now a trio of gentlemen
from neighboring lands arrives—a condolence call from Eliphaz,
Bildad, and Zophar, Job's distinguished old friends. The three
weep and are mute—Job's broken figure appalls: pitiable, desolate, dusted with ash, scraped, torn.

All the foregoing is told in the plain prose of a folktale: a blameless man's undoing through the conniving of a mischievous sprite. A prose epilogue will ultimately restore Job to his good fortune, and in the arbitrary style of a fable, will even double it; but between the two halves of this simple narrative of loss and restitution, the coloration of legend falls away, and a majesty of outcry floods speech after speech. And then Job's rage ascends—a rage against the loathsomeness of "wisdom."

When the horrified visitors regain their voices, it is they who appear to embody reasonableness, logic, and prudence, while Job—introduced in the prologue as a man of steadfast faith who will never affront the Almighty—rails like a blasphemer against an unjust God. The three listen courteously as Job bewails the day he was born, a day that "did not shut the doors of my mother's womb, nor hide trouble from my eyes." In response to which, Eliphaz begins his first attempt at solace: "Can mortal man be righteous before God? Can a man be pure before his Maker? . . . Behold, happy is the man whom God reproves; therefore despise not the chastening of the Almighty." Here is an early and not altogether brutal hint of what awaits Job in the severer discourse of his consolers: the logic of punishment, the dogma of requital. If a man suffers, it must be because of some impiety he has committed. Can Job claim that he is utterly without sin? And is not God a merciful God, "for he wounds, but he binds up; he smites, but his hands heal"? In the end, Eliphaz reassures Job, all will be well.

Job is not comforted; he is made furious. He has been accused, however obliquely, of having sinned, and he knows with his whole soul that he has not. His friends show themselves to be as inconstant as a torrential river, icy in winter, vanishing away in the heat. Rather than condole, they defame. They root amelioration in besmirchment. But if Job's friends are no friends, then what of God? The poet, remembering the Psalm—"What is man that thou are mindful of him?"—has Job echo the very words. "What is man," Job charges God, that "thou dost set thy mind upon him, dost visit him every morning, and test him every moment? . . . If I sin, what do I do to thee, thou watcher of men?" And he dreams of escaping God in death: "For now I shall lie in the earth; thou wilt seek me, but I shall not be."

Three rounds of increasingly tumultuous debate follow, with Eliphaz, Bildad, and Zophar each having a turn, and Job replying. Wilder and wilder grow the visitors' accusations; wilder and wilder grow Job's rebuttals, until they are pitched into an abyss of bitterness. Job's would-be comforters have become his harriers; men of standing themselves, they reason from the conventional doctrines of orthodox religion, wherein conduct and consequence are morally linked: goodness rewarded, wickedness punished. No matter how hotly Job denies and protests, what greater proof of Job's impiety can there be than his deadly ordeal? God is just; he metes out just deserts. Is this not the grand principle on which the world rests?

Job's own experience refutes these arguments; and his feverish condemnation of God's injustice refutes religion itself. "I am blameless!" he cries yet again, and grimly concludes: "It is all one: therefore I say, he destroys both the blameless and the wicked. When disaster brings sudden death, he mocks at the calamity of the innocent. The earth is given into the hand of the wicked; he covers the face of its judges." Here Job, remarkably, is both believer and atheist. God's presence is incontrovertible; God's moral integrity is nil. And how strange: in the heart of Scripture, a righteous man impugning God! Genesis, to be sure, records what appears to be a precedent. "Wilt thou destroy the righteous with the wicked?" Abraham asks God when Sodom's fate is at stake; but that is more plea than indictment, and anyhow there is no innocence in Sodom. Yet how distant Job is from the Psalmist who sings, "The Lord is upright . . . there is no unrighteousness in him," who pledges that "the righteous shall flourish like the palm tree," and "the workers of iniquity shall be destroyed forever." The Psalmist's is the voice of faith. Job's is the voice of a wounded lover, betrayed.

Like a wounded lover, he envisions, fleetingly, a forgiving afterlife, the way a tree, cut down to a stump, can send forth new shoots and live again—while man, by contrast, "lies down and rises not again." Or he imagines the workings of true justice: on the one hand, he wishes he might bring God himself to trial; on the other, he ponders man-made law and its courts, and declares that the transcript of his testimony ought to be inscribed permanently in stone, so that some future clansman might one day come as a vindicator, to proclaim the probity of Job's case. (Our translation famously renders the latter as "I know that my Redeemer lives," a phrase that has, of course, been fully integrated into Christian hermeneutics.) Throughout, there is a thundering of discord and clangor. "Miserable comforters are you all!" Job groans. "Surely there are mockers about me"—while Eliphaz, Bildad, and Zophar press on, from pious apologias to uncontrolled denunciation. You, Job, they accuse, you who stripped the naked of their clothing, gave no water to the weary, withheld bread from the hungry!

And Job sees how the tenets of rectitude, in the mouths of the zealous, are perverted to lies.

But now, abruptly, a new voice is heard: a fifth and so far undisclosed player strides onstage. He is young, intellectually ingenious, confident, a bit brash. Unlike the others, he bears a name with a Hebrew ring to it: Elihu. "I also will declare my opinion," he announces. He arrives as a supplanter, to replace stale wisdom with fresh, and begins by rebuking Job's haranguers for their dogma of mechanical tit for tat. As for Job: in his recalcitrance, in

his litanies of injured innocence, in his prideful denials, he has
been blind to the *uses* of suffering; and doesn't he recognize that
God manifests himself in night visions and dreams? Suffering
educates and purifies; it humbles pride, tames the rebel, corrects
the scoffer. "What man is like Job, who drinks up scoffing like
water?" Elihu points out—but here the reader detects a logical
snag. Job has become a scoffer only as a result of gratuitous suffering: then how is such suffering a "correction" of scoffing that
never was? Determined though he is to shake Job's obstinacy,
Elihu is no wiser than his elders. Job's refusal of meaningless
chastisement stands.

So Elihu, too, fails as a comforter—but as he leaves off suasion,
his speech metamorphoses into a hymn in praise of God's dominion. "Hear this, O Job," Elihu calls, "stop and consider the won-
drous works of God"—cloud, wind, sky, snow, lightning, ice!
Elihu's sumptuous limning of God's power in nature is a fore-
echo of the sublime climax to come.

The Voice out of the Whirlwind

Job, gargantuan figure in the human imagination that he is, is not
counted among the prophets. He is not the first to be reluctant to
accept God's authority: Jonah rebelled against sailing to Nineveh
in order to prophesy; yet he did go, and his going was salvational
for a people not his own. But the true prophets are self-starters,
spontaneous fulminators against social inequity, and far from
reluctant. Job, then, has much in common with Isaiah, Jeremiah,
Micah, and Amos: he is wrathful that the wicked go unpunished,
that the widow and the orphan go unsuccored, that the world is
not clothed in righteousness. Like the noblest of prophets, he
assails injustice; and still he is unlike them. They accuse the men
and women who do evil; their targets are made of flesh and blood.

It is human transgression they hope to mend. Job seeks to rectify God. His is an ambition higher, deeper, vaster, grander than theirs; he is possessed by a righteousness more frenzied than theirs; the scale of his justice-hunger exceeds all that precedes him, all that was ever conceived; he can be said to be the consummate prophet. And at the same time he is the consummate violator. If we are to understand him at all, if we are rightly to enter into his passions at their pinnacle, then we ought to name him prophet; but we may not. Call him, instead, antiprophet—his teaching, after all, verges on atheism: the rejection of God's power. His thesis is revolution.

Eliphaz, Bildad, and Zophar are silenced. Elihu will not strut these boards again. Job's revolution may be vanity of vanities, but his adversaries have lost confidence and are scattered. Except for Job, the stage is emptied.

Then God enters—not in a dream, as Elihu theorized, not as a vision or incarnation, but as an irresistible Eloquence.

Here I am obliged to remark on the obvious. In recapitulating certain passages, I have reduced an exalted poem to ordinary spoken sentences. But the ideas that buttress Job are not merely expressed in, as we say, language of high beauty; they are inseparable from an artistry so far beyond the grasp of mind and tongue that one can hardly imagine their origin. We think of the Greek plays; we think of Shakespeare; and still that is not marvel enough. Is it that the poet is permitted to sojourn, for the poem's brief life, in the magisterial Eye of God? Or is it God who allows himself to peer through the poet's glass, as through a gorgeously crafted kaleidoscope? The words of the poem are preternatural, unearthly. They may belong to a rhapsodic endowment so rare as to appear among mortals only once in three thousand years. Or they may belong to the Voice that hurls itself from the whirlwind.

The Answer

God has granted Job's demand: "Let the Almighty answer me!" Now here at last is Job's longed-for encounter with that Being he conceives to be his persecutor. What is most extraordinary in this visitation is that it appears to be set apart from everything that has gone before. What is the Book of Job *about*? It is about gratuitous affliction. It is about the wicked who escape whipping. It is about the suffering of the righteous. God addresses none of this. It is as if he has belatedly stepped into the drama having not consulted the script—none of it: not even so much as the prologue. He does not remember Satan's mischief. He does not remember Job's calamities. He does not remember Job's righteousness.

As to the last: Job will hardly appeal for an accounting from God without first offering one of his own. He has his own credibility to defend, his own probity. "Let me be weighted in a just balance," he insists, "and let God know my integrity!" The case for his integrity takes the form of a bill of particulars that is unsurpassed as a compendium of compassionate human conduct: no conceivable ethical nuance is omitted. It is as if all the world's moral fervor, distilled from all the world's religions, and touching on all the world's pain, is assembled in Job's roster of loving-kindness. Job in his confession of integrity is both a protector and a lover of God's world.

But God seems alarmingly impatient; his mind is elsewhere. Is this the Lord whom Job once defined as a "watcher of men"? God's answer, a fiery challenge, roils out of the whirlwind. "Where were *you*," the Almighty roars, in supernal strophes that blaze through the millennia, "when I laid the foundation of the earth?" And what comes crashing and tumbling out of the gale is an exuberant ode to the grandeur of the elements, to the fecundity of nature: the sea and the stars, the rain and the dew, the constellations in their courses, the lightning, the lion, the raven, the goat, the ass, the ostrich, the horse, the hawk—and more, more, more! The lavishness, the extravagance, the infinitude! An infinitude of power; an infinitude of joy; an infinitude of love, even for the ugly hippopotamus, even for the crocodile with his terrifying teeth, even for creatures made mythical through ancient lore. Even for the Leviathan! Nothing in the universe is left unpraised in these glorious stanzas—and one thinks: had the poet access to the electrons, had he an inkling of supernovas, had he parsed the chains of DNA, God's ode to Creation could not be richer. Turn it and turn it—God's ode: everything is in it.

Everything but the answer to the question that eats at Job's soul: why God permits injustice in the fabric of a world so resplendently woven. Job is conventionally judged to be a moral violator because he judges God himself to be a moral violator. Yet is there any idea in the history of human thought more exquisitely tangled, more furiously daring, more heroically courageous, more rooted in spirit and conscience than Job's question? Why does God not praise the marrow of such a man as Job at least as much as he praises the intricacy of the crocodile's scales? God made the crocodile; he also made Job.

God's answer to Job lies precisely in his not answering; and Job, with lightning insight, comprehends. "I have uttered what I did not understand," he acknowledges, "things too wonderful for me, which I did not know."

His new knowledge is this: that a transcendent God denies us a god of our own devising, a god that we would create out of our own malaise, or complaint, or desire, or hope, or imagining; or would manufacture according to the satisfaction of our own design. We are part of God's design: can the web manufacture the spider? The Voice out of the whirlwind warns against god-manufacture—against the degradation of a golden calf surely,

but also against god-manufacture even in the form of the loft-
iest visions. Whose visions are they? Beware: they are not God's;
they are ours. The ways of the true God cannot be penetrated.
The false comforters cannot decipher them. Job cannot uncover
them. "The secret things belong to the Lord our God," Job's poet
learned long ago, reading Deuteronomy. But now: see how Job
cannot draw Leviathan out with a hook—how much less can he
draw out God's nature, and his purpose!

So the poet, through the whirlwind's answer, stills Job.

But can the poet still the Job who lives in us? God's majesty is
eternal, manifest in cell and star. Yet Job's questions toil on, manifest in death camp and hatred, in tyranny and anthrax, in bomb
and bloodshed. Why do the wicked thrive? Why do the innocent
suffer? In brutal times, the whirlwind's answer tempts, if not
atheism, then the sorrowing conviction of God's indifference.

And if we are to take the close of the tale as given, it is not only
Job's protests that are stilled; it is also his inmost moral urge. What
has become of raging conscience? What has become of loving-
kindness? Prosperity is restored; the dead children are replaced
by twice the number of boys, and by girls exceedingly comely. But
where now is the father's bitter grief over the loss of those earlier
sons and daughters, on whose account he once indicted God?
Cushioned again by good fortune, does Job remember nothing,
feel nothing, see nothing beyond his own renewed honor? Is Job's
lesson from the whirlwind finally no more than the learning of
indifference?

So much for the naked text. Perhaps this is why—century after
century—we common readers go on clinging to the spiritualizing
mentors of traditional faith, who clothe in comforting theologies
this God-wrestling and comfortless book.

Yet how astoundingly up-to-date they are, those ancient sages—

redactors and compilers—who opened even the sacred gates of Scripture to philosophic doubt!

Note: In preparing these reflections, I am particularly indebted to *The Book of God and Man: A Study of Job,* by Robert Gordis (Chicago: University of Chicago Press, 1965); and to *Where Shall Wisdom Be Found? Calvin's Exegesis of Job from Medieval and Modern Perspectives,* by Susan E. Schreiner (Chicago: University of Chicago Press, 1994).

The Book *of* Job

Chapter 1

There was a man in the land of Uz, whose name was Job; and that man was blameless and upright, one who feared God, and turned away from evil. There were born to him seven sons and three daughters. He had seven thousand sheep, three thousand camels, five hundred yoke of oxen, and five hundred she-asses, and very many servants; so that this man was the greatest of all the people of the east. His sons used to go and hold a feast in the house of each on his day; and they would send and invite their three sisters to eat and drink with them. And when the days of the feast had run their course, Job would send and sanctify them, and he would rise early in the morning and offer burnt offerings according to the number of them all; for Job said, "It may be that my sons have sinned, and cursed God in their hearts." Thus Job did continually.

Now there was a day when the sons of God came to present themselves before the Lord, and Satan also came among them. The Lord said to Satan, "Whence have you come?" Satan answered the Lord, "From going to and fro on the earth, and from walking up and down on it." And the Lord said to Satan, "Have you considered my servant Job, that there is none like him on the earth, a blameless and upright man, who fears God and turns away from evil?" Then Satan answered the Lord, "Does Job fear God for nought? Hast thou not put a hedge about him and his house and all that he has, on every side? Thou hast blessed the work of his hands, and his possessions have increased in the land. But put forth thy hand now, and touch all that he has, and he will curse thee to thy face." And the Lord said to Satan, "Behold, all that he has is in your power; only upon himself do not

THE BOOK OF JOB

put forth your hand." So Satan went forth from the presence of the Lord.

Now there was a day when his sons and daughters were eating and drinking wine in their eldest brother's house; and there came a messenger to Job, and said, "The oxen were plowing and the asses feeding beside them; and the Sabeans fell upon them and took them, and slew the servants with the edge of the sword; and I alone have escaped to tell you." While he was yet speaking, there came another, and said, "The fire of God fell from heaven and burned up the sheep and the servants, and consumed them; and I alone have escaped to tell you." When he was yet speaking, there came another, and said, "The Chaldeans formed three companies, and made a raid upon the camels and took them, and slew the servants with the edge of the sword, and I alone have escaped to tell you." While he was yet speaking, there came another, and said, "Your sons and daughters were eating and drinking wine in their eldest brother's house; and behold, a great wind came across the wilderness, and struck the four corners of the house, and it fell upon the young people, and they are dead; and I alone have escaped to tell you."

Then Job arose, and rent this robe, and shaved his head, and fell upon the ground, and worshiped. And he said, "Naked I came from my mother's womb, and naked shall I return; the Lord gave, and the Lord has taken away; blessed be the name of the Lord."

In all this Job did not sin or charge God with wrong.

Chapter 2

Again there was a day when the sons of God came to present themselves before the Lord, and Satan also came among them to present himself before the Lord. And the Lord said to Satan, "Whence have you come?" Satan answered the Lord, "From going to and fro on the earth, and from walking up and down upon it." And the Lord said to Satan, "Have you considered my servant Job, that there is none like him on earth, a blameless and upright man, who fears God and turns away from evil? He still holds fast his integrity, although you moved me against him, to destroy him without cause." Then Satan answered the Lord, "Skin for skin! All that a man has he will give for his life. But put forth thy hand now, and touch his bone and his flesh, and he will curse thee to thy face." And the Lord said to Satan, "Behold, he is in your power; only spare his life."

So Satan went forth from the presence of the Lord, and afflicted Job with loathsome sores from the sole of his foot to the crown of his head. And he took a potsherd with which to scrape himself, and sat among the ashes.

Then his wife said to him, "Do you still hold fast your integrity? Curse God, and die." But he said to her, "You speak as one of the foolish women would speak. Shall we receive good at the hand of God, and shall we not receive evil?" In all this Job did not sin with his lips.

Now when Job's three friends heard all this evil that had come upon him, they came each from his own place, Eliphaz the Temanite, Bildad the Shuhite, and Zophar the Naamathite. They made an appointment together to come to condole with him and comfort him. And when they saw him from afar, they did not recognize him; and they raised their voices and wept; and they rent their robes and sprinkled dust upon their heads toward heaven. And they sat with him on the ground seven days and seven nights, and no one spoke a word to him, for they saw that his suffering was very great.

Chapter 3

After this Job opened his mouth and cursed the day of his birth.
And Job said:

"Let the day perish wherein I was born,
    and the night which said, 'A man-child is conceived.'
Let that day be darkness!
    May God above not seek it, nor light shine upon it.
Let gloom and deep darkness claim it.
    Let clouds dwell upon it; let the blackness of the day terrify it.
That night—let thick darkness seize it!
    let it not rejoice among the days of the year,
        let it not come into the number of the months.
Yea, let that night be barren;
    let no joyful cry be heard in it.
    Let those who curse it curse the day,
        who are skilled to rouse the Leviathan.
Let the stars of its dawn be dark;
        let it hope for light, but have none,
        nor see the eyelids of the morning;
    because it did not shut the doors of my mother's womb,
        nor hide trouble from my eyes.

"Why did I not die at birth,
    come forth from the womb and expire?
    Why did the knees receive me?
Or why the breasts, that I should suck?
    For then I should have lain down and been quiet;
        I should have slept; then I should have been at rest,
with kings and counselors of the earth
    who rebuilt ruins for themselves,

or with princes who had gold,
    who filled their houses with silver.
Or why was I not as a hidden untimely birth,
    as infants that never see the light?
There the wicked cease from troubling,
    and there the weary are at rest.
There the prisoners are at ease together;
    they hear not the voice of the taskmaster.
The small and the great are there,
    and the slave is free from his master.

"Why is light given to him that is in misery,
    and life to the bitter in soul,
who long after death, but it comes not,
    and dig for it more than for hid treasures;
who rejoice exceedingly,
    and are glad, when they find the grave?
Why is light given to a man whose way is hid,
    whom God has hedged in?
For my sighing comes as my bread,
    and my groanings are poured out like water.
For the thing that I fear comes upon me,
    and what I dread befalls me.
I am not at ease, nor am I quiet; I have no rest,
    but trouble comes."

Chapter 4

Then Eliphaz the Temanite answered:

"If one ventures a word with you, will you be offended?
    Yet who can keep from speaking?

Behold, you have instructed many,
  and you have strengthened the weak hands.
  Your words have upheld him who was stumbling,
    and you have made firm the feeble knees.
But now it has come to you, and you are impatient;
    it touches you, and you are dismayed.
  Is not your fear of God your confidence,
    and the integrity of your ways your hope?

"Think now, who that was innocent ever perished?
  Or where were the upright cut off?
As I have seen, those who plow iniquity
    and sow trouble reap the same.
  By the breath of God they perish,
    and by the blast of his anger they are consumed.
The roar of the lion, the voice of the fierce lion,
    the teeth of the young lions, are broken.
  The strong lion perishes for lack of prey,
    and the whelps of the lioness are scattered.

"Now a word was brought to me stealthily,
    my ear received the whisper of it.
  Amid thoughts from visions of the night,
    when deep sleep falls on men,
    dread came upon me, and trembling,
    which made all my bones shake.
A spirit glided past my face;
    the hair of my flesh stood up.
  It stood still,
    but I could not discern its appearance.
A form was before my eyes;

there was silence, then I heard a voice:
  'Can mortal man be righteous before God?
Can a man be pure before his Maker?
  Even in his servants he puts no trust,
    and his angels he charges with error;
how much more those who dwell in houses of clay,
    whose foundation is in the dust,
    who are crushed before the moth.
  Between morning and evening they are destroyed;
    they perish forever without any regarding it.
If their tent-cord is plucked up within them,
    do they not die, and that without wisdom?'

Chapter 5

"Call now, is there anyone who will answer you?
  To which of the holy ones will you turn?
Surely vexation kills the fool,
    and jealousy slays the simple.
  I have seen the fool taking root,
    but suddenly I cursed his dwelling.
His sons are far from safety,
    they are crushed in the gate,
    and there is no one to deliver them.
  His harvest the hungry eat,
    and he takes it even out of thorns;
    and the thirsty pant after his wealth.
For affliction does not come from the dust,
    nor does trouble start from the ground;

but man is born to trouble
    as the sparks fly upward.

"As for me, I would seek God,
    and to God would I commit my cause;
  who does great things and unsearchable,
    marvelous things without number:
he gives rain upon the earth
    and sends water upon the fields;
  he sets on high those who are lowly,
    and those who mourn are lifted to safety.
He frustrates the devices of the crafty,
    so that their hands achieve no success.
  He takes the wise in their own craftiness;
    and the schemes of the wily are brought to a quick end.
They meet with darkness in the daytime,
    and grope at noonday as in the night.
  But he saves the fatherless from their mouth,
    the needy from the hand of the mighty.
So the poor have hope,
    and injustice shuts her mouth.

"Behold, happy is the man whom God reproves;
    therefore despise not the chastening of the Almighty.
  For he wounds, but he binds up;
    he smites, but his hands heal.
He will deliver you from six troubles;
    in seven there shall no evil touch you.
  In famine he will redeem you from death,
    and in war from the power of the sword.
You shall be hid from the scourge of the tongue,
    and shall not fear destruction when it comes.

At destruction and famine you shall laugh,
and shall not fear the beasts of the earth.
For you shall be in league with the stones of the field,
and the beasts of the field shall be at peace with you.
You shall know that your tent is safe,
and you shall inspect your fold and miss nothing.
You shall know also that your descendants shall be many,
and your offspring as the grass of the earth.
You shall come to your grave in ripe old age,
as a shock of grain comes up to the threshing floor
in its season.
Lo, this we have searched out; it is true.
Hear, and know it for your good."

Chapter 6

Then Job answered:

"O that my vexation were weighed,
and all my calamity laid in the balances!
For then it would be heavier than the sand of the sea;
therefore my words have been rash.
For the arrows of the Almighty are in me;
my spirit drinks their poison;
the terrors of God are arrayed against me.
Does the wild ass bray when he has grass,
or the ox low over his fodder?
Can that which is tasteless be eaten without salt,
or is there any taste in the slime of the purslane?
My appetite refuses to touch them;
they are food that is loathsome to me.

"O that I might have my request,
 and that God would grant my desire;
 that it would please God to crush me,
  that he would let loose his hand and cut me off!
This would be my consolation;
 I would even exult in pain unsparing;
 for I have not denied the words of the Holy One.
What is my strength, that I should wait?
 And what is my end, that I should be patient?
Is my strength the strength of stones,
 or is my flesh bronze?
 In truth I have no help in me,
  and any resource is driven from me.

"He who withholds kindness from a friend
 forsakes the fear of the Almighty.
 My brethren are as treacherous as a torrent-bed,
  as freshets that pass away,
which are dark with ice,
 and where the snow hides itself.
 In time of heat they disappear;
  when it is hot, they vanish from their place.
The caravans turn aside from their course;
 they go up into the waste, and perish.
 The caravans of Tema look,
  the travelers of Sheba hope.
They are disappointed because they were confident;
 they come thither and are confounded.
 Such you have now become to me;
  you see my calamity, and are afraid.
Have I said, 'Make me a gift'?
 Or, 'From your wealth offer a bribe for me'?

Or, 'Deliver me from the adversary's hand'?
Or, 'Ransom me from the hand of oppressors'?

"Teach me, and I will be silent;
make me understand how I have erred.
How forceful are honest words!
But what does reproof from you reprove?
Do you think that you can reprove words,
when the speech of a despairing man is wind?
You would even cast lots over the fatherless,
and bargain over your friend.

"But now, be pleased to look at me;
for I will not lie to your face.
Turn, I pray, let no wrong be done.
Turn now, my vindication is at stake.
Is there any wrong on my tongue?
Cannot my taste discern calamity?

Chapter 7

"Has not man a hard service upon earth,
and are not his days like the days of a hireling?
Like a slave who longs for the shadow,
and like a hireling who looks for his wages,
so I am allotted months of emptiness,
and nights of misery are apportioned to me.
When I lie down I say, 'When shall I arise?'
But the night is long,
and I am full of tossing till the dawn.

My flesh is clothed with worms and dirt;
    my skin hardens, then breaks out afresh.
  My days are swifter than a weaver's shuttle,
    and come to their end without hope.

"Remember that my life is a breath;
    my eye will never again see good.
  The eye of him who sees me will behold me no more;
    while thy eyes are upon me, I shall be gone.
As the cloud fades and vanishes,
    so he who goes down to Sheol does not come up;
he returns no more to his house,
    nor does his place know him anymore.

"Therefore I will not restrain my mouth;
    I will speak in the anguish of my spirit;
    I will complain in the bitterness of my soul.
  Am I the sea, or a sea monster,
    that thou settest a guard over me?
When I say, 'My bed will comfort me,
    my couch will ease my complaint,'
  then thou dost scare me with dreams
    and terrify me with visions,
so that I would choose strangling
    and death rather than my bones.
  I loathe my life; I would not live forever.
Let me alone, for my days are a breath.
  What is a man, that thou dost make so much of him,
    and that thou dost set thy mind upon him,
dost visit him every morning,
    and test him every moment?
  How long wilt thou not look away from me,

nor let me alone till I swallow my spittle?
 If I sin, what do I do to thee, thou watcher of men?
Why hast thou made me thy mark?
 Why have I become a burden to thee?
Why dost thou not pardon my transgression
  and take away my iniquity?
 For now I shall lie in the earth;
  thou wilt seek me, but I shall not be."

Chapter 8

Then Bildad the Shuhite answered:

"How long will you say these things,
  and the words of your mouth be a great wind?
 Does God pervert justice?
Or does the Almighty pervert the right?
 If your children have sinned against him,
  he has delivered them into the power of their transgression.
If you will seek God
  and make supplication to the Almighty,
 if you are pure and upright,
  surely then he will rouse himself for you
  and reward you with a rightful habitation.
And though your beginning was small,
  your latter days will be very great.

"For inquire, I pray you, of bygone ages,
  and consider what the fathers have found;
 for we are but of yesterday, and know nothing,
  for our days on earth are a shadow.

Will they not teach you, and tell you,
>and utter words out of their understanding?

"Can papyrus grow where there is no marsh?
>Can reeds flourish where there is no water?
While yet in flower and not cut down,
>they wither before any other plant.
>Such are the paths of all who forget God;
>the hope of the godless man shall perish.
His confidence breaks in sunder,
>and his trust is a spider's web.
He leans against his house, but it does not stand;
>he lays hold of it, but it does not endure.
He thrives before the sun,
>and his shoots spread over his garden.
>His roots twine about the stone-heap;
>he lives among the rocks.
If he is destroyed from his place,
>then it will deny him, saying, 'I have never seen you.'
>Behold, this is the joy of his way;
>and out of the earth others will spring.

"Behold, God will not reject a blameless man,
>nor take the hand of evildoers.
He will yet fill your mouth with laughter,
>and your lips with shouting.
Those who hate you will be clothed with shame,
>and the tent of the wicked will be no more."

Chapter 9

Then Job answered:

"Truly I know that it is so:
    But how can a man be just before God?
If one wished to contend with him,
        one could not answer him once in a thousand times.
    He is wise in heart, and mighty in strength—
who has hardened himself against him, and succeeded?—
    he who removes mountains, and they know it not,
        when he overturns them in his anger;
who shakes the earth out of its place,
        and its pillars tremble;
    who commands the sun, and it does not rise;
        who seals up the stars;
who alone stretched out the heavens,
        and trampled the waves of the sea;
    who made the Bear and Orion,
        the Pleiades and the chambers of the south;
who does great things beyond understanding,
        and marvelous things without number.
    Lo, he passes by me, and I see him not;
        he moves on, but I do not perceive him.
Behold, he snatches away; who can hinder him?
    Who will say to him, 'What doest thou?'

"God will turn back his anger;
        beneath him bowed the helpers of Rahab.
    How then can I answer him,
        choosing my words with him?

Though I am innocent, I cannot answer him;
    I must appeal for mercy to my accuser.
  If I summoned him and he answered me,
    I would not believe that he was listening to my voice.
For he crushes me with a tempest,
    and multiplies my wounds without cause;
  he will not let me get my breath,
    but fills me with bitterness.
If it is a contest of strength, behold him!
  If it is a matter of justice, who can summon him?
Though I am innocent, my own mouth would condemn me;
    though I am blameless, he would prove me perverse.
  I am blameless; I regard not myself;
    I loathe my life.
It is all one; therefore I say,
    he destroys both the blameless and the wicked.
  When disaster brings sudden death,
    he mocks at the calamity of the innocent.
The earth is given into the hand of the wicked;
    he covers the faces of its judges—
  if it is not he, who then is it?

"My days are swifter than a runner;
    they flee away, they see no good.
  They go by like skiffs of reed,
    like an eagle swooping on the prey.
If I say, 'I will forget my complaint,
    I will put off my sad countenance, and be of good cheer,'
  I become afraid of all my suffering,
    for I know thou wilt not hold me innocent.
I shall be condemned;
    why then do I labor in vain?

If I wash myself with snow,
　　and cleanse my hands with lye,
yet thou wilt plunge me into a pit,
　　and my own clothes will abhor me.
　For he is not a man, as I am, that I might answer him,
　　that we should come to trial together.
There is no umpire between us,
　　who might lay his hand upon us both.
　Let him take his rod away from me,
　　and let not dread of him terrify me.
Then I would speak without fear of him,
　　for I am not so in myself.

Chapter 10

"I loathe my life;
　I will give free utterance to my complaint;
I will speak in the bitterness of my soul.
　I will say to God, Do not condemn me;
　　let me know why thou dost contend against me.
Does it seem good to thee to oppress,
　　to despise the work of thy hands
　　and favor the designs of the wicked?
　Hast thou eyes of flesh?
　　Dost thou see as man sees?
Are thy days as the days of man,
　　or thy years as man's years?
　that thou dost seek out my iniquity
　　and search for my sin,
although thou knowest that I am not guilty,
　　and there is none to deliver out of thy hand?

Thy hands fashioned and made me;
    and now thou dost turn about and destroy me.
Remember that thou hast made me of clay;
    and wilt thou turn me to dust again?
  Didst thou not pour me out like milk
    and curdle me like cheese?
Thou didst clothe me with skin and flesh,
    and knit me together with bones and sinews.
  Thou hast granted me life and steadfast love;
    and thy care has preserved my spirit.
Yet these things thou didst hide in thy heart;
    I know that this was thy purpose.
  If I sin, thou dost mark me,
    and dost not acquit me of my iniquity.
If I am wicked, woe to me!
    If I am righteous, I cannot lift up my head,
  for I am filled with disgrace
    and look upon my affliction.
And if I lift myself up, thou dost hunt me like a lion,
    and again work wonders against me;
  thou dost renew thy witnesses against me,
    and increase thy vexation toward me;
    thou dost bring fresh hosts against me.

"Why didst thou bring me forth from the womb?
    Would that I had died before any eye had seen me,
  and were as though I had not been,
    carried from the womb to the grave.
Are not the days of my life few?
    Let me alone, that I might find a little comfort
  before I go whence I shall not return,
    to the land of gloom and deep darkness,

the land of gloom and chaos,
    where light is as darkness."

Chapter 11

Then Zophar the Naamathite answered:

"Should a multitude of words go unanswered,
    and a man full of talk be vindicated?
  Should your babble silence men,
    and when you mock, shall no one shame you?
For you say, 'My doctrine is pure,
    and I am clean in God's eyes.'
  But oh, that God would speak,
    and open his lips to you,
and that he would tell you the secrets of wisdom!
    For he is manifold in understanding.
  Know then that God exacts of you
    less than your guilt deserves.

"Can you find out the deep things of God?
    Can you find out the limit of the Almighty?
  It is higher than heaven—what can you do?
    Deeper than Sheol—what can you know?
Its measure is longer than the earth,
    and broader than the sea.
  If he passes through, and imprisons,
    and calls to judgment, who can hinder him?
For he knows worthless men;
    when he sees iniquity, will he not consider it?

But a stupid man will get understanding,
    when a wild ass's colt is born a man.

"If you set your heart aright,
    you will stretch out your hands toward him.
If iniquity is in your hand, put it far away,
    and let not wickedness dwell in your tents.
Surely then you will lift up your face without blemish;
    you will be secure, and will not fear.
You will forget your misery;
    you will remember it as waters that have passed away.
And your life will be brighter than the noonday;
    its darkness will be like the morning.
And you will have confidence, because there is hope;
    you will be protected and take your rest in safety.
You will lie down, and none will make you afraid;
    many will entreat your favor.
But the eyes of the wicked will fail;
    all way of escape will be lost to them,
and their hope is to breathe their last."

Chapter 12

Then Job answered:

"No doubt you are the people,
    and wisdom will die with you.
But I have understanding as well as you;
    I am not inferior to you.
Who does not know such things as these?
    I am a laughingstock to my friends;

I, who called upon God and he answered me,
    a just and blameless man, am a laughingstock.
  In the thought of one who is at ease
      there is contempt for misfortune;
      it is ready for those whose feet slip.
The tents of robbers are at peace,
    and those who provoke God are secure,
    who bring their god in their hand.

"But ask the beasts, and they will teach you;
    the birds of the air, and they will tell you;
  or the plants of the earth, and they will teach you;
    and the fish of the sea will declare to you.
Who among all these does not know
    that the hand of the Lord has done this?
  In his hand is the life of every living thing
    and the breath of all mankind.
Does not the ear try words
    as the palate tastes food?
  Wisdom is with the aged,
    and understanding in length of days.

"With God are wisdom and might;
    he has counsel and understanding.
  If he tears down, none can rebuild;
    if he shuts a man in, none can open.
If he withholds the waters, they dry up;
    if he sends them out, they overwhelm the land.
  With him are strength and wisdom;
    the deceived and the deceiver are his.
He leads counselors away stripped,
    and judges he makes fools.

He looses the bonds of kings,
    and binds a waistcloth on their loins.
He leads priests away stripped,
    and overthrows the mighty.
He deprives of speech those who are trusted,
    and takes away the discernment of the elders.
He pours contempt on princes,
    and looses the belt of the strong.
He uncovers the deeps out of darkness,
    and brings deep darkness to light.
He makes nations great, and he destroys them:
    he enlarges nations, and leads them away.
He takes away understanding from the chiefs of the people
    of the earth,
and makes them wander in a pathless waste.
    They grope in the dark without light;
    and he makes them stagger like a drunken man.

Chapter 13

"Lo, my eye has seen all this,
    my ear has heard and understood it.
What you know, I also know;
    I am not inferior to you.
But I would speak to the Almighty,
    and I desire to argue my case with God.
As for you, you whitewash with lies;
    worthless physicians are you all.
Oh, that you would keep silent,
    and it would be your wisdom!

Hear now my reasoning,
    and listen to the pleadings of my lips.
Will you speak falsely for God,
    and speak deceitfully for him?
    Will you show partiality toward him,
    will you plead the case for God?
Will it be well with you when he searches you out?
    Or can you deceive him, as one deceives a man?
    He will surely rebuke you
    if in secret you show partiality.
Will not his majesty terrify you,
    and the dread of him fall upon you?
    Your maxims are proverbs of ashes,
    your defenses are defenses of clay.

"Let me have silence, and I will speak,
    and let come on me what may.
    I will take my flesh in my teeth,
    and put my life in my hand.
Behold, he will slay me; I have no hope;
    yet I will defend my ways to his face.
    This will be my salvation,
    that a godless man shall not come before him.
Listen carefully to my words,
    and let my declaration be in your ears.
    Behold, I have prepared my case;
    I know that I shall be vindicated.
Who is there that will contend with me?
    For then I would be silent and die.
    Only grant two things to me,
    then I will not hide myself from thy face:

Withdraw thy hand far from me,
 and let not dread of thee terrify me.
 Then call, and I will answer;
  or let me speak, and do thou reply to me.
How many are my iniquities and my sins?
  Make me know my transgression and my sin.
 Why dost thou hide thy face,
  and count me as thy enemy?
Wilt thou frighten a driven leaf
  and pursue dry chaff?
 For thou writest bitter things against me,
  and makest me inherit the iniquities of my youth.
Thou puttest my feet in the stocks,
  and watchest all my paths;
  thou settest a bound to the soles of my feet.
 Man wastes away like a rotten thing,
  like a garment that is moth-eaten.

Chapter 14

"Man that is born of a woman is of few days,
  and full of trouble.
 He comes forth like a flower, and withers;
  he flees like a shadow, and continues not.
And dost thou open thy eyes upon such a one
  and bring him into judgment with thee?
 Who can bring a clean thing out of an unclean?
  There is not one.
Since his days are determined,
  and the number of his months is with thee,
  and thou hast appointed his bounds that he cannot pass,

look away from him, and desist,
>that he may enjoy, like a hireling, his day.

"For there is hope for a tree,
>if it be cut down, that it will sprout again,
>and its shoots will not cease.
>Though its root grow old in the earth,
>and its stump die in the ground,
yet at the scent of water it will bud
>and put forth branches like a young plant.
>But man dies, and is laid low;
>man breathes his last, and where is he?
As waters fail from a lake,
>and a river wastes away and dries up,
>so man lies down and rises not again;
>till the heavens are no more he will not awake,
>or be roused out of his sleep.
Oh that thou wouldest hide me in Sheol,
>that thou wouldest conceal me until thy wrath be past,
>that thou wouldest appoint me a set time, and remember me!
If a man die, shall he live again?
>All the days of my service I would wait,
>till my release should come.
Thou wouldest call, and I would answer thee;
>thou wouldest long for the work of thy hands.
>For then thou wouldest number my steps,
>thou wouldest not keep watch over my sin;
my transgression would be sealed up in a bag,
>and thou wouldest cover over my iniquity.

"But the mountain falls and crumbles away,
>and the rock is removed from its place;

the waters wear away the stones;
    the torrents wash away the soil of the earth;
so thou destroyest the hope of man.
    Thou prevailest forever against him, and he passes;
thou changest his countenance, and sendest him away.
    His sons come to honor, and he does not know it;
they are brought low, and he perceives it not.
    He feels only the pain of his own body,
    and he mourns only for himself."

Chapter 15

Then Eliphaz the Temanite answered:

"Should a wise man answer with windy knowledge,
    and fill himself with the east wind?
Should he argue in unprofitable talk,
    or in words with which he can do no good?
But you are going away with the fear of God,
    and hindering meditation before God.
For your iniquity teaches your mouth,
    and you choose the tongue of the crafty.
Your own mouth condemns you, and not I;
    your own lips testify against you.

"Are you the first man that was born?
    Or were you brought forth before the hills?
Have you listened in the council of God?
    And do you limit wisdom to yourself?
What do you know that we do not know?
    What do you understand that is not clear to us?

Both the gray-haired and the aged are among us,
  older than your father.
Are the consolations of God too small for you,
  or the word that deals gently with you?
Why does your heart carry you away,
  and why do your eyes flash,
that you turn your spirit against God,
  and let such words go out of your mouth?
What is man, that he can be clean?
  Or he that is born of a woman, that he can be righteous?
Behold, God puts no trust in his holy ones,
  and the heavens are not clean in his sight;
  how much less one who is abominable and corrupt,
  a man who drinks iniquity like water!

"I will show you, hear me;
  and what I have seen I will declare
(what wise men have told,
  and their fathers have not hidden,
to whom alone the land was given,
  and no stranger passed among them).
The wicked man writhes in pain all his days,
  through all the years that are laid up for the ruthless.
Terrifying sounds are in his ears;
  in prosperity the destroyer will come upon him.
He does not believe that he will return out of darkness,
  and he is destined for the sword.
He wanders abroad for bread, saying 'Where is it?'
  He knows that a day of darkness is ready at his hand;
  distress and anguish terrify him;
  they prevail against him, like a king prepared for battle.

Because he has stretched forth his hand against God,
    and bids defiance to the Almighty,
  running stubbornly against him
    with a thick-bossed shield;
because he has covered his face with his fat,
    and gathered fat upon his loins,
  and has lived in desolate cities,
    in houses which no man should inhabit,
    which were destined to become heaps of ruins;
he will not be rich, and his wealth will not endure,
    nor will he strike root in the earth;
  he will not escape from darkness;
    the flame will dry up his shoots,
    and his blossom will be swept away by the wind.
Let him not trust in emptiness, deceiving himself;
    for emptiness will be his recompense.
It will be paid in full before his time,
    and his branch will not be green.
He will shake off his unripe grape, like the vine,
    and cast off his blossoms, like the olive tree.
  For the company of the godless is barren,
    and fire consumes the tents of bribery.
They conceive mischief and bring forth evil
    and their heart prepares deceit."

Chapter 16

Then Job answered:

"I have heard many such things;
    miserable comforters are you all.

Shall windy words have an end?
　　Or what provokes you that you answer?
I also could speak as you do,
　　if you were in my place;
　　I could join words together against you,
　　　　and shake my head at you.
I could strengthen you with my mouth,
　　and the solace of my lips would assuage your pain.

"If I speak, my pain is not assuaged,
　　and if I forbear, how much of it leaves me?
　　Surely now God has worn me out;
　　　　he has made desolate all my company.
And he has shriveled me up,
　　which is a witness against me;
　　and my leanness has risen up against me,
　　　　it testifies to my face.
He has torn me in his wrath, and hated me; he has
　　gnashed his teeth at me;
　　my adversary sharpens his eyes against me.
　　Men have gaped at me with their mouth,
　　　　they have struck me insolently upon the cheek,
　　　　they mass themselves together against me.
God gives me up to the ungodly,
　　and casts me into the hands of the wicked.
　　I was at ease, and he broke me asunder;
　　　　he seized me by the neck and dashed me to pieces;
he set me up as his target, his archers surround me.
　　He slashes open my kidneys, and does not spare;
　　　　he pours out my gall on the ground.
He breaks me with breach upon breach;
　　he runs upon me like a warrior.

I have sewed sackcloth upon my skin,
    and have laid my strength in the dust.
My face is red with weeping,
    and on my eyelids is deep darkness;
    although there is no violence in my hands,
    and my prayer is pure.

"O earth, cover not my blood,
    and let my cry find no resting place.
    Even now, behold, my witness is in heaven,
    and he that vouches for me is on high.
My friends scorn me;
    my eye pours out tears to God,
    that he would maintain the right of a man with God,
    like that of a man with his neighbor.
For when a few years have come
    I shall go the way whence I shall not return.

Chapter 17

"My spirit is broken, my days are extinct,
    the grave is ready for me.
    Surely there are mockers about me,
    and my eye dwells on their provocation.

"Lay down a pledge for me with thyself;
    who is there that will give surety for me?
    Since thou hast closed their minds to understanding,
    therefore thou wilt not let them triumph.
He who informs against his friends
    to get a share of their property,
    the eyes of his children will fail.

"He has made me a byword of the peoples,
and I am one before whom men spit.
My eye has grown dim from grief,
and all my members are like a shadow.
Upright men are appalled at this,
and the innocent stirs himself up against the godless.
Yet the righteous holds to his way,
and he that has clean hands grows stronger and stronger.
But you, come on again, all of you,
and I shall not find a wise man among you.
My days are past, my plans are broken off,
the desires of my heart.
They make night into day;
'The light,' they say, 'is near to the darkness.'
If I look for Sheol as my house,
if I spread my couch in darkness,
if I say to the pit, 'You are my father,'
and to the worm, 'My mother,' or 'My sister,'
where then is my hope?
Who will see my hope?
Will it go down to the bars of Sheol?
Shall we descend together into the dust?"

Chapter 18

Then Bildad the Shuhite answered:

"How long will you hunt for words?
Consider, and then we will speak.
Why are we counted as cattle?
Why are we stupid in your sight?

You who tear yourself in your anger,
>> shall the earth be forsaken for you,
>> or the rock be removed out of its place?

"Yea, the light of the wicked is put out,
>> and the flame of his fire does not shine.
> The light is dark in his tent,
>> and his lamp above him is put out.
His strong steps are shortened
>> and his own schemes throw him down.
> For he is cast into a net by his own feet,
>> and he walks on a pitfall.
A trap seizes him by the heel,
>> a snare lays hold of him.
> A rope is hid for him in the ground,
>> a trap for him in the path.
Terrors frighten him on every side,
>> and chase him at his heels.
> His strength is hunger-bitten,
>> and calamity is ready for his stumbling.
By disease his skin is consumed,
>> the first-born of death consumes his limbs.
> He is torn from the tent in which he trusted,
>> and is brought to the king of terrors.
In his tent dwells that which is none of his;
>> brimstone is scattered upon his habitation.
> His roots dry up beneath,
>> and his branches wither above.
His memory perishes from the earth,
>> and he has no name in the street.
> He is thrust from light to darkness,
>> and driven out of the world.

He has no offspring or descendant among his people,
and no survivor where he used to live.
They of the west are appalled at his day,
and horror seizes them of the east.
Surely such are the dwellings of the ungodly,
such is the place of him who knows not God."

Chapter 19

Then Job answered:

"How long will you torment me,
and break me in pieces with words?
These ten times you have cast reproach upon me;
are you not ashamed to wrong me?
And even if it be true that I have erred,
my error remains with myself.
If indeed you magnify yourselves against me,
and make my humiliation an argument against me,
know then that God has put me in the wrong,
and closed his net about me.
Behold, I cry out, 'Violence!' but I am not answered;
I call aloud, but there is no justice.
He has walled up my way, so that I cannot pass,
and he has set darkness upon my paths.
He has stripped from me my glory,
and taken the crown from my head.
He breaks me down on every side, and I am gone,
and my hope has he pulled up like a tree.
He has kindled his wrath against me,
and counts me as his adversary.

His troops come on together;
>they have cast up siegeworks against me,
>and encamp round about my tent.

"He has put my brethren far from me,
>and my acquaintances are wholly estranged from me.
>My kinsfolk and my close friends have failed me;
>the guests in my house have forgotten me;
my maidservants count me as a stranger;
>I have become an alien in their eyes.
>I call to my servant, but he gives no answer;
>I must beseech him with my mouth.
I am repulsive to my wife,
>loathsome to the sons of my own mother.
>Even young children despise me;
>when I rise they talk against me.
All my intimate friends abhor me,
>and those whom I loved have turned against me.
>My bones cleave to my skin and to my flesh,
>and I have escaped by the skin of my teeth.
Have pity on me, have pity on me, O you my friends,
>for the hand of God has touched me!
>Why do you, like God, pursue me?
>Why are you not satisfied with my flesh?

"Oh that my words were written!
>Oh that they were inscribed in a book!
>Oh that with an iron pen and lead
>they were graven in the rock forever!
For I know that my Redeemer lives,
>and at last he will stand upon the earth;

and after my skin has been thus destroyed,
    then from my flesh I shall see God,
Whom I shall see on my side,
    and my eyes shall behold, and not another.
    My heart faints within me!
If you say, 'How we will pursue him!'
    and, 'The root of the matter is found in him';
    be afraid of the sword,
      for wrath brings the punishment of the sword,
      that you may know there is a judgment."

Chapter 20

Then Zophar the Naamathite answered:

"Therefore my thoughts answer me
    because of my haste within me.
  I hear censure which insults me
    and out of my understanding a spirit answers me.
Do you not know this from of old,
    since man was placed upon earth,
  that the exulting of the wicked is short,
    and the joy of the godless but for a moment?
Though his height mount up to the heavens,
    and his head reach to the clouds,
  he will perish for ever like his own dung;
    those who have seen him will say, 'Where is he?'
He will fly away like a dream, and not be found;
    he will be chased away like a vision of the night.
  The eye which saw him will see him no more,
    nor will his place any more behold him.

His children will seek the favor of the poor,
and his hands will give back his wealth.
His bones are full of youthful vigor,
but it will lie down with him in the dust.

"Though wickedness is sweet in his mouth,
though he hides it under his tongue,
though he is loath to let it go,
and holds it in his mouth,
yet his food is turned in his stomach;
it is the gall of asps within him.
He swallows down riches and vomits them up again;
God casts them out of his belly.
He will suck the poison of asps;
the tongue of a viper will kill him.
He will not look upon the rivers,
the streams flowing with honey and curds.
He will give back the fruit of his toil,
and will not swallow it down;
from the profit of his trading
he will get no enjoyment.
For he has crushed and abandoned the poor,
he has seized a house which he did not build.

"Because his greed knew no rest,
he will not save anything in which he delights.
There was nothing left after he had eaten;
therefore his prosperity will not endure.
In the fullness of his sufficiency he will be in straits;
all the force of misery will come upon him.
To fill his belly to the full
God will send his fierce anger into him,

and rain it upon him as his food.
He will flee from an iron weapon;
    a bronze arrow will strike him through.
  It is drawn forth and comes out of his body,
    the glittering point comes out of his gall;
    terrors come upon him.
Utter darkness is laid up for his treasures;
    a fire not blown upon will devour him;
    what is left in his tent will be consumed.
  The heavens will reveal his iniquity,
    and the earth will rise up against him.
The possessions of his house will be carried away,
    dragged off in the day of God's wrath.
  This is the wicked man's portion from God,
    the heritage decreed for him by God."

Chapter 21

Then Job answered:

"Listen carefully to my words,
    and let this be your consolation.
  Bear with me, and I will speak,
    and after I have spoken, mock on.
As for me, is my complaint against man?
    Why should I not be impatient?
  Look at me, and be appalled,
    and lay your hand upon your mouth.
When I think of it I am dismayed,
    and shuddering seizes my flesh.
  Why do the wicked live,

reach old age, and grow mighty in power?
Their children are established in their presence,
and their offspring before their eyes.
Their houses are safe from fear,
and no rod of God is upon them.
Their bull breeds without fail;
their cow calves, and does not cast her calf.
They send forth their little ones like a flock,
and their children dance.
They sing to the tambourine and the lyre,
and rejoice to the sound of the pipe.
They spend their days in prosperity,
and in peace they go down to Sheol.
They say to God, 'Depart from us!
We do not desire the knowledge of thy ways.
What is the Almighty, that we should serve him?
And what profit do we get if we pray to him?'
Behold, is not their prosperity in their hand?
The counsel of the wicked is far from me.

"How often is it that the lamp of the wicked is put out?
That their calamity comes upon them?
That God distributes pains in his anger?
That they are like straw before the wind,
and like chaff that the storm carries away?
You say, 'God stores up their iniquity for their sons.'
Let him recompense it to themselves, that they may know it.
Let their own eyes see their destruction,
and let them drink of the wrath of the Almighty.
For what do they care for their houses after them,
when the number of their months is cut off?

Will any teach God knowledge,
  seeing that he judges those that are on high?
One dies in full prosperity,
  being wholly at ease and secure,
his body full of fat
  and the marrow of his bones moist.
Another dies in bitterness of soul,
  never having tasted of good.
They lie down alike in the dust,
  and worms cover them.

"Behold, I know your thoughts,
  and your schemes to wrong me.
For you say, 'Where is the house of the prince?
  Where is the tent in which the wicked dwelt?'
Have you not asked those who travel the roads,
  and do you not accept their testimony
that the wicked man is spared in the day of calamity,
  that he is rescued in the day of wrath?
Who declares his way to his face,
  and who requites him for what he has done?
When he is borne to the grave,
  watch is kept over his tomb.
The clods of the valley are sweet to him;
  all men follow after him,
  and those who go before him are innumerable.
How then will you comfort me with empty nothings?
  There is nothing left of your answers but falsehood."

Chapter 22

Then Eliphaz the Temanite answered:

"Can a man be profitable to God?
    Surely he who is wise is profitable to himself.
  Is it any pleasure to the Almighty if you are righteous,
      or is it gain to him if you make your ways blameless?
Is it for your fear of him that he reproves you,
      and enters into judgment with you?
  Is not your wickedness great?
      There is no end to your iniquities.
For you have exacted pledges of your brothers for nothing,
      and stripped them naked of their clothing.
  You have given no water to the weary to drink,
      and you have withheld bread from the hungry.
The man with power possessed the land,
      and the favored man dwelt in it.
  You have sent widows away empty,
      and the arms of the fatherless were crushed.
Therefore snares are round about you,
      and sudden terror overwhelms you;
    your light is darkened, so that you cannot see,
      and a flood of water covers you.

"Is not God high in the heavens?
    See the highest stars, how lofty they are!
  Therefore you say, 'What does God know?
    Can he judge through the deep darkness?
Thick clouds enwrap him, so that he does not see,
      and he walks on the vault of heaven.'

Will you keep to the old way
    which wicked men have trod?
They were snatched away before their time;
    their foundation was washed away.
    They said to God, 'Depart from us,'
      and, 'What can the Almighty do to us?'
Yet he filled their houses with good things—
    but the counsel of the wicked is far from me.
    The righteous see it and are glad;
      the innocent laugh them to scorn,
saying, 'Surely our adversaries are cut off,
    and what they left the fire has consumed.'

"Agree with God and be at peace;
    thereby good will come to you.
    Receive instruction from his mouth,
      and lay up his words in your heart.
If you return to the Almighty and humble yourself,
    if you remove unrighteousness far from your tents,
    if you lay gold in the dust,
      and gold of Ophir among the stones of the torrent bed,
and if the Almighty is your gold,
    and your precious silver;
    then you will delight yourself in the Almighty,
      and lift up your face to God.
You will make your prayer to him,
    and he will hear you;
    and you will pay your vows.
    You will decide on a matter, and it will be established for you,
      and light will shine on your ways.
For God abases the proud,
    but he saves the lowly.

He delivers the innocent man;
>you will be delivered through the cleanness of your hands."

Chapter 23

Then Job answered:

"Today also my complaint is bitter,
>his hand is heavy in spite of my groaning.
>Oh, that I knew where I might find him,
>>that I might come even to his seat!
I would lay my case before him,
>and fill my mouth with arguments.
>I would learn what he would answer me,
>>and understand what he would say to me.
Would he contend with me in the greatness of his power?
>No; he would give heed to me.
>There an upright man could reason with him,
>>and I should be acquitted for ever by my judge.

"Behold, I go forward, but he is not there;
>and backward, but I cannot perceive him;
on the left hand I seek him, but I cannot behold him;
>I turn to the right hand, but I cannot see him.
But he knows the way that I take;
>when he has tried me, I shall come forth as gold.
My foot has held fast to his steps;
>I have kept his way and have not turned aside.
I have not departed from the commandment of his lips;
>I have treasured in my bosom the words of his mouth.

But he is unchangeable and who can turn him?
    What he desires, that he does.
For he will complete what he appoints for me;
    and many such things are in his mind.
Therefore I am terrified at his presence;
    when I consider, I am in dread of him.
God has made my heart faint;
    the Almighty has terrified me;
for I am hemmed in by darkness,
    and thick darkness covers my face.

Chapter 24

"Why are not times of judgment kept by the Almighty,
    and why do those who know him never see his days?
Men remove landmarks;
    they seize flocks and pasture them.
They drive away the ass of the fatherless;
    they take the widow's ox for a pledge.
They thrust the poor off the road;
    the poor of the earth all hide themselves.
Behold, like wild asses in the desert
    they go forth to their toil,
seeking prey in the wilderness
    as food for their children.
They gather their fodder in the field
    and they glean the vineyard of the wicked man.
They lie all night naked, without clothing,
    and have no covering in the cold.
They are wet with the rain of the mountains,
    and cling to the rock for want of shelter.

(There are those who snatch the fatherless child
    from the breast,
    and take in pledge the infant of the poor.)
  They go about naked, without clothing;
    hungry, they carry the sheaves;
among the olive rows of the wicked they make oil;
    they tread the wine presses, but suffer thirst.
  From out of the city the dying groan,
    and the soul of the wounded cries for help;
yet God pays no attention to their prayer.

"There are those who rebel against the light,
    who are not acquainted with its ways,
    and do not stay in its paths.
  The murderer rises in the dark,
    that he may kill the poor and needy;
    and in the night he is as a thief.
The eye of the adulterer also waits for the twilight,
    saying, 'No eye will see me';
    and he disguises his face.
  In the dark they dig through houses;
    by day they shut themselves up;
    they do not know the light.
For deep darkness is morning to all of them;
    for they are friends with the terrors of deep darkness.

"You say, 'They are swiftly carried away
    upon the face of the waters;
    their portion is cursed in the land;
    no treader turns toward their vineyards.
  Drought and heat snatch away the snow waters;

so does Sheol those who have sinned.
The squares of the town forget them;
>their name is no longer remembered;
>so wickedness is broken like a tree.'

"They feed on the barren childless woman,
>and do no good to the widow.
>Yet God prolongs the life of the mighty by his power;
>they rise up when they despair of life.
He gives them security, and they are supported;
>and his eyes are upon their ways.
>They are exalted a little while, and then are gone;
>they wither and fade like the mallow;
>they are cut off like the heads of grain.
If it is not so, who will prove me a liar,
>and show that there is nothing in what I say?"

Chapter 25

Then Bildad the Shuhite answered:

"Dominion and fear are with God;
>he makes peace in his high heaven.
>Is there any number to his armies?
>Upon whom does his light not arise?
How then can man be righteous before God?
>How can he who is born of woman be clean?
>Behold, even the moon is not bright
>and the stars are not clean in his sight;

how much less man, who is a maggot,
    and the son of man, who is a worm!"

Chapter 26

Then Job answered:

"How you have helped him who has no power!
    How you have saved the arm that has no strength!
How you have counseled him who has no wisdom,
    and plentifully declared sound knowledge!
    With whose help have you uttered words,
    and whose spirit has come forth from you?
The shades below tremble,
    the waters and their inhabitants.
    Sheol is naked before God,
    and Abaddon has no covering.
He stretches out the north over the void,
    and hangs the earth upon nothing.
    He binds up the waters in his thick clouds,
    and the cloud is not rent under them.
He covers the face of the moon,
    and spreads over it his cloud.
    He has described a circle upon the face of the waters
    at the boundary between light and darkness.
The pillars of heaven tremble,
    and are astounded at his rebuke.
    By his power he stilled the sea;
    by his understanding he smote Rahab.
By his wind the heavens were made fair;
    his hand pierced the fleeing serpent.

Lo, these are but the outskirts of his ways;
    and how small a whisper do we hear of him!
But the thunder of his power who can understand?"

Chapter 27

And Job again took up his discourse, and said:

"As my God lives, who has taken away my right,
    and the Almighty, who has made my soul bitter;
  as long as my breath is in me,
    and the spirit of God is in my nostrils;
my lips will not speak falsehood,
    and my tongue will not utter deceit.
  Far be it from me to say that you are right;
    till I die I will not put away my integrity from me.
I hold fast my righteousness, and will not let it go;
    my heart does not reproach me for any of my days.

"Let my enemy be as the wicked,
    and let him that rises up against me be as the unrighteous.
  For what is the hope of the godless when God cuts him off,
    when God takes away his life?
Will God hear his cry,
    when trouble comes upon him?
  Will he take delight in the Almighty?
  Will he call upon God at all times?
I will teach you concerning the hand of God;
    what is with the Almighty I will not conceal.
  Behold, all of you have seen it yourselves;
    why then have you become altogether vain?

"This is the portion of a wicked man with God,
and the heritage which oppressors
receive from the Almighty:
If his children are multiplied, it is for the sword;
and his offspring have not enough to eat.
Those who survive him the pestilence buries,
and their widows make no lamentation.
Though he heap up silver like dust,
and pile up clothing like clay;
he may pile it up, but the just will wear it,
and the innocent will divide the silver.
The house which he builds is like a spider's web,
like a booth which a watchman makes.
He goes to bed rich, but will do so no more;
he opens his eyes, and his wealth is gone.
Terrors overtake him like a flood;
in the night a whirlwind carries him off.
The east wind lifts him up and he is gone;
it sweeps him out of his place.
It hurls at him without pity;
he flees from its power in headlong flight.
It claps its hands at him,
and hisses at him from its place.

Chapter 28

"Surely there is a mine for silver,
and a place for gold which they refine.
Iron is taken out of the earth,
and copper is smelted from the ore.

Men put an end to darkness,
    and search out to the farthest bound
    the ore in gloom and deep darkness.
  They open shafts in a valley away from where men live;
    they are forgotten by travelers,
    they hang afar from men, they swing to and fro.
As for the earth, out of it comes bread;
    but underneath it is turned up as by fire.
  Its stones are the place of sapphires,
    and it has the dust of gold.

"That path no bird of prey knows,
    and the falcon's eye has not seen it.
  The proud beasts have not trodden it;
    the lion has not passed over it.

"Man puts his hand to the flinty rock,
    and overturns mountains by the roots.
  He cuts out channels in the rocks,
    and his eye sees every precious thing.
He binds up the streams so that they do not trickle,
    and the thing that is hid he brings forth to light.

"But where shall wisdom be found?
    And where is the place of understanding?
  Man does not know the way to it,
    and it is not found in the land of the living.
The deep says, 'It is not in me,'
    and the sea says, 'It is not with me.'
  It cannot be gotten for gold,
    and silver cannot be weighed as its price.

It cannot be valued in the gold of Ophir,
    in precious onyx or sapphire.
  Gold and glass cannot equal it,
    nor can it be exchanged for jewels of fine gold.
No mention shall be made of coral or of crystal;
    the price of wisdom is above pearls.
  The topaz of Ethiopia cannot compare with it,
    nor can it be valued in pure gold.

"Whence then comes wisdom?
    And where is the place of understanding?
  It is hid from the eyes of all living,
    and concealed from the birds of the air.
Abaddon and Death say,
    'We have heard a rumor of it with our ears.'

"God understands the way to it,
    and he knows its place.
  For he looks to the ends of the earth,
    and sees everything under the heavens.
When he gave to the wind its weight,
    and meted out the waters by measure;
  when he made a decree for the rain,
    and a way for the lightning of the thunder;
then he saw it and declared it;
    he established it, and searched it out.
  And he said to man,
    'Behold, the fear of the Lord, that is wisdom;
    and to depart from evil is understanding.' "

Chapter 29

And Job again took up his discourse, and said:

"Oh, that I were as in the months of old,
    as in the days when God watched over me;
  when his lamp shone upon my head,
    and by his light I walked through darkness;
as I was in my autumn days,
    when the friendship of God was upon my tent;
  when the Almighty was yet with me,
    when my children were about me;
when my steps were washed with milk,
    and the rock poured out for me streams of oil!
  When I went out to the gate of the city,
    when I prepared my seat in the square,
the young men saw me and withdrew,
    and the aged rose and stood;
  the princes refrained from talking,
    and laid their hand on their mouth;
the voice of the nobles was hushed,
    and their tongue cleaved to the roof of their mouth.
  When the ear heard, it called me blessed,
    and when the eye saw, it approved;
because I delivered the poor who cried,
    and the fatherless who had none to help him.
  The blessing of him who was about to perish came upon me,
    and I caused the widow's heart to sing for joy.
I put on righteousness, and it clothed me;
    my justice was like a robe and a turban.
  I was eyes to the blind,
    and feet to the lame.

I was a father to the poor,
    and I searched out the cause of him whom I did
      not know.
  I broke the fangs of the unrighteous,
    and made him drop his prey from his teeth.
Then I thought, 'I shall die in my nest,
    and I shall multiply my days as the sand,
  my roots spread out of the waters,
    with the dew all night on my branches,
my glory fresh with me,
    and my bow ever new in my hand.'

"Men listened to me, and waited,
    and kept silence for my counsel.
  After I spoke they did not speak again,
    and my word dropped upon them.
They waited for me as for the rain;
    and they opened their mouths as for the spring rain.
  I smiled on them when they had no confidence;
    and the light of my countenance they did not
      cast down.
I chose their way, and sat as chief,
    and I dwelt like a king among his troops,
    like one who comforts mourners.

Chapter 30

"But now they make sport of me,
    men who are younger than I,
  whose fathers I would have disdained
    to set with the dogs of my flock.

What could I gain from the strength of their hands,
    men whose vigor is gone?
  Through want and hard hunger
    they gnaw the dry and desolate ground;
they pick mallow and the leaves of bushes,
    and to warm themselves the roots of the broom.
  They are driven out from among men;
    they shout after them as after a thief.
In the gullies of the torrents they must dwell,
    in the holes of the earth and of the rocks.
  Among the bushes they bray;
    under the nettles they huddle together.
A senseless, a disreputable brood,
    they have been whipped out of the land.

"And now I have become their song,
    I am a byword to them.
  They abhor me, they keep aloof from me;
    they do not hesitate to spit at the sight of me.
Because God has loosed my cord and humbled me,
    they have cast off restraint in my presence.
  On my right hand the rabble rise,
    they drive me forth,
    they cast up against me their ways of destruction.
They break up my path,
    they promote my calamity;
    no one restrains them.
  As through a wide breach they come;
    amid the crash they roll on.
Terrors are turned upon me;
    my honor is pursued as by the wind,
    and my prosperity has passed away like a cloud.

"And now my soul is poured out within me;
    days of affliction have taken hold of me.
  The night racks my bones,
    and the pain that gnaws me takes no rest.
With violence it seizes my garment;
    it binds me about like the collar of my tunic.
  God has cast me into the mire,
    and I have become like dust and ashes.
I cry to thee and thou dost not answer me;
    I stand, and thou dost not heed me.
  Thou hast turned cruel to me;
    with the might of thy hand thou dost persecute me.
Thou liftest me up on the wind, thou makest me ride on it,
    and thou tossest me about in the roar of the storm.
  Yea, I know that thou wilt bring me to death,
    and to the house appointed for all living.

"Yet does not one in a heap of ruins stretch out his hand,
    and in his disaster cry for help?
  Did I not weep for him whose day was hard?
    Was not my soul grieved for the poor?
But when I looked for good, evil came;
    and when I waited for light, darkness came.
  My heart is in turmoil, and is never still;
    days of affliction come to meet me.
I go about blackened, but not by the sun;
    I stand up in the assembly, and cry for help.
  I am a brother of jackals,
    and a companion of ostriches.
My skin turns black and falls from me,
    and my bones burn with heat.

My lyre is turned to mourning,
    and my pipe to the voice of those who weep.

Chapter 31

"I have made a covenant with my eyes;
    how then could I look upon a virgin?
What would be my portion from God above,
    and my heritage from the Almighty on high?
Does not calamity befall the unrighteous,
    and disaster the workers of iniquity?
Does not he see my ways,
    and number all my steps?

"If I have walked with falsehood,
    and my foot has hastened to deceit;
(Let me be weighed in a just balance,
    and let God know my integrity!)
if my step has turned aside from the way,
    and my heart has gone after my eyes,
    and if any spot has cleaved to my hands;
then let me sow, and another eat;
    and let what grows for me be rooted out.

"If my heart has been enticed to a woman,
    and I have lain in wait at my neighbor's door;
then let my wife grind for another,
    and let others bow down upon her.
For that would be a heinous crime;
    that would be an iniquity to be punished by the judges;

for that would be a fire which consumes unto Abaddon,
    and it would burn to the root my increase.

"If I have rejected the cause of my manservant or my maidservant,
    when they brought a complaint against me;
what then shall I do when God rises up?
    When he makes inquiry, what shall I answer him?
Did not he who made me in the womb make him?
    And did not one fashion us in the womb?

"If I have withheld anything that the poor desired,
    or have caused the eyes of the widow to fail,
or have eaten my morsel alone,
    and the fatherless has not eaten of it
(for from his youth I reared him as a father,
    and from his mother's womb I guided him);
if I have seen any one perish for lack of clothing,
    or a poor man without covering;
if his loins have not blessed me,
    and if he was not warmed with the fleece of my sheep;
if I have raised my hand against the fatherless,
    because I saw help in the gate;
then let my shoulder blade fall from my shoulder,
    and let my arm be broken from its socket.
For I was in terror of calamity from God,
    and I could not have faced his majesty.

"If I have made gold my trust,
    or called fine gold my confidence;
if I have rejoiced because my wealth was great,
    or because my hand had gotten much;

if I have looked at the sun when it shone,
    or the moon moving in splendor,
  and my heart has been secretly enticed,
    and my mouth has kissed my hand;
this also would be an iniquity to be punished by the judges,
    for I should have been false to God above.

"If I have rejoiced at the ruin of him that hated me,
    or exulted when evil overtook him
  (I have not let my mouth sin
    by asking for his life with a curse);
if the men of my tent have not said,
    'Who is there that has not been filled with his meat?'
  (the sojourner has not lodged in the street;
    I have opened my doors to the wayfarer);
if I have concealed my transgressions from men,
    by hiding iniquity in my bosom,
  because I stood in great fear of the multitude,
    and the contempt of families terrified me,
    so that I kept silence and did not go out of doors—
  Oh, that I had one to hear me!
  (Here is my signature! let the Almighty answer me!)
Oh, that I had the indictment written by my adversary!
  Surely I would carry it on my shoulder;
    I would bind it on me as a crown;
I would give him an account of all my steps;
    like a prince I would approach him.

"If my land has cried out against me,
    and its furrows have wept together;
  if I have eaten its yield without payment,

and caused the death of its owners;
let thorns grow instead of wheat,
and foul weeds instead of barley."

The words of Job are ended.

Chapter 32

So these three men ceased to answer Job, because he was righteous in his own eyes. Then Elihu the son of Barachel the Buzite,
of the family of Ram, became angry. He was angry at Job because
he justified himself rather than God; he was angry also at Job's
three friends because they had found no answer, although they
had declared Job to be in the wrong. Now Elihu had waited to
speak to Job because they were older than he. And when Elihu
saw that there was no answer in the mouth of these three men, he
became angry.

And Elihu the son of Barachel the Buzite answered:

"I am young in years,
and you are aged;
therefore I was timid and afraid
to declare my opinion to you.
I said, 'Let days speak,
and many years teach wisdom.'
But it is the spirit in a man,
the breath of the Almighty,
that makes him understand.
It is not the old that are wise,
nor the aged that understand what is right.

Therefore I say, 'Listen to me;
   let me also declare my opinion.'

"Behold, I waited for your words.
   I listened for your wise sayings,
      while you searched out what to say.
   I gave you my attention,
      and, behold, there was none that confuted Job,
      or that answered his words, among you.
Beware lest you say, 'We have found wisdom;
   God may vanquish him, not man.'
   He has not directed his words against me,
      and I will not answer him with your speeches.

"They are discomfited, they answer no more;
   they have not a word to say.
   And shall I wait, because they do not speak,
      because they stand there and answer no more?
I also will give my answer;
   I also will declare my opinion.
   For I am full of words,
      the spirit within me constrains me.
Behold, my heart is like wine that has no vent;
   like new wineskins, it is ready to burst.
   I must speak, that I may find relief;
      I must open my lips and answer.
I will not show partiality to any person,
   or use flattery toward any man.
   For I do not know how to flatter,
      else would my Maker soon put an end to me.

Chapter 33

"But now, hear my speech, O Job,
>and listen to all my words.
>Behold, I open my mouth;
>>the tongue in my mouth speaks.
My words declare the uprightness of my heart,
>and what my lips know they speak sincerely.
>The spirit of God has made me,
>and the breath of the Almighty gives me life.
Answer me, if you can;
>set your words in order before me; take your stand.
>Behold, I am toward God as you are;
>I too was formed from a piece of clay.
Behold, no fear of me need terrify you;
>my pressure will not be heavy upon you.

"Surely, you have spoken in my hearing,
>and I have heard the sound of your words.
>You say, 'I am clean, without transgression;
>I am pure, and there is no iniquity in me.
Behold, he finds occasions against me,
>he counts me as his enemy;
>he puts my feet in the stocks,
>>and watches all my paths.'

"Behold, in this you are not right. I will answer you.
>God is greater than man.
>Why do you contend against him,
>saying, 'He will answer none of my words'?
For God speaks in one way,
>and in two, though man does not perceive it.

In a dream, in a vision of the night,
  when deep sleep falls upon men,
  while they slumber on their beds,
then he opens the ears of men,
  and terrifies them with warnings,
  that he may turn man aside from his deed,
  and cut off pride from man;
he keeps back his soul from the Pit,
  his life from perishing by the sword.

"Man is also chastened with pain upon his bed,
  and with continual strife in his bones;
  so that his life loathes bread,
  and his appetite dainty food.
His flesh is so wasted away that it cannot be seen;
  and his bones which were not seen stick out.
  His soul draws nearer to the Pit,
  and his life to those who bring death.
If there be for him an angel,
  a mediator, one of the thousand,
  to declare to man what is right for him;
  and he is gracious to him, and says,
  'Deliver him from going down into the Pit,
  I have found a ransom;
let his flesh become fresh with youth;
  let him return to the days of his youthful vigor';
  then man prays to God, and he accepts him,
  he comes into his presence with joy.
He recounts to men his salvation,
  and he sings before men, and says:
  'I sinned, and perverted what was right,
  and it was not requited to me.

He has redeemed my soul from going down into the Pit,
    and my light shall see the light.'

"Behold, God does all these things,
    twice, three times, with a man,
  to bring back his soul from the Pit,
    that he may see the light of life.
Give heed, O Job, listen to me;
    be silent, and I will speak.
  If you have anything to say, answer me;
    speak, for I desire to justify you.
If not, listen to me;
    be silent, and I will teach you wisdom."

Chapter 34

Then Elihu said:

"Hear my words, you wise men,
    and give ear to me, you who know;
  for the ear tests words
    as the palate tastes food.
Let us choose what is right;
    let us determine among ourselves what is good.
  For Job has said, 'I am innocent,
    and God has taken away my right;
in spite of my right I am counted a liar;
    my wound is incurable, though I am without trans-
    gression.'
  What man is like Job,
    who drinks up scoffing like water,

who goes in company with evildoers
  and walks with wicked men?
 For he has said, 'It profits a man nothing
   that he should take delight in God.'

"Therefore, hear me, you men of understanding,
  far be it from God that he should do wickedness,
and from the Almighty that he should do wrong.
 For according to the work of a man he will requite him,
and according to his ways he will make it befall him.
 Of a truth, God will not do wickedly,
   and the Almighty will not pervert justice.
Who gave him charge over the earth
   and who laid on him the whole world?
 If he should take back his spirit to himself,
   and gather to himself his breath,
all flesh would perish together,
   and man would return to dust.

"If you have understanding, hear this;
   listen to what I say.
 Shall one who hates justice govern?
   Will you condemn him who is righteous and mighty,
who says to a king, 'Worthless one,'
   and to nobles, 'Wicked man';
 who shows no partiality to princes,
   nor regards the rich more than the poor,
   for they are all the work of his hands?
In a moment they die;
   at midnight the people are shaken and pass away,
   and the mighty are taken away by no human hand.

"For his eyes are upon the ways of a man,
    and he sees all his steps.
  There is no gloom or deep darkness
    where evildoers may hide themselves.
For he has not appointed a time for any man
    to go before God in judgment.
He shatters the mighty without investigation,
    and sets others in their place.
Thus, knowing their works,
    he overturns them in the night, and they are crushed.
He strikes them for their wickedness
    in the sight of men,
because they turned aside from following him,
    and had no regard for any of his ways,
  so that they caused the cry of the poor to come to him,
    and he heard the cry of the afflicted—
When he is quiet, who can condemn?
    When he hides his face, who can behold him,
    whether it be a nation or a man?—
that a godless man should not reign,
    that he should not ensnare the people.

"For has anyone said to God,
    'I have borne chastisement; I will not offend any more;
  teach me what I do not see;
    if I have done iniquity, I will do it no more'?
Will he then make requital to suit you,
    because you reject it?
  For you must choose, and not I;
    therefore declare what you know.
Men of understanding will say to me,
    and the wise man who hears me will say:

'Job speaks without knowledge,
    his words are without insight.'
Would that Job were tried to the end,
    because he answers like wicked men.
  For he adds rebellion to his sin;
    he claps his hands among us,
      and multiplies his words against God."

Chapter 35

And Elihu said:

"Do you think this to be just?
    Do you say, 'It is my right before God,'
  that you ask, 'What advantage have I?
    How am I better off than if I had sinned?'
I will answer you,
    and your friends with you.
  Look at the heavens, and see;
    and behold the clouds, which are higher than you.
If you have sinned, what do you accomplish against him?
  And if your transgressions are multiplied,
    what do you do to him?
If you are righteous, what do you give to him;
    or what does he receive from your hand?
  Your wickedness concerns a man like yourself,
    and your righteousness a son of man.

"Because of the multitude of oppressions people cry out;
    they call for help because of the arm of the mighty.

But none says, 'Where is God my Maker,
    who gives songs in the night,
who teaches us more than the beasts of the earth,
    and makes us wiser than the birds of the air?'
There they cry out, but he does not answer,
    because of the pride of evil men.
Surely God does not hear an empty cry,
    nor does the Almighty regard it.
How much less when you say that you do not see him,
    that the case is before him, and you are waiting for him!
And now, because his anger does not punish,
    and he does not greatly heed transgression,
Job opens his mouth in empty talk,
    he multiplies words without knowledge."

Chapter 36

And Elihu continued, and said:

"Bear with me a little, and I will show you,
    for I have yet something to say on God's behalf.
I will fetch my knowledge from afar,
    and ascribe righteousness to my Maker.
For truly my words are not false;
    one who is perfect in knowledge is with you.

"Behold, God is mighty, and does not despise any;
    he is mighty in strength and understanding.
He does not keep the wicked alive,
    but gives the afflicted their right.

He does not withdraw his eyes from the righteous,
    but with kings upon the throne
    he sets them for ever, and they are exalted.
  And if they are bound in fetters,
    and caught in the cords of affliction,
then he declares to them their work
    and their transgressions, that they are behaving arrogantly.
  He opens their ears to instruction,
    and commands that they return from iniquity.
If they hearken and serve him,
    they complete their days in prosperity,
    and their years in pleasantness.
  But if they do not hearken, they perish by the sword,
    and die without knowledge.

"The godless in heart cherish anger;
    they do not cry for help when he binds them.
  They die in youth,
    and their life ends in shame.
He delivers the afflicted by their affliction,
    and opens their ear by adversity.
  He also allured you out of distress
    into a broad place where there was no cramping,
and what was set on your table was full of fatness.

"But you are full of the judgment on the wicked;
    judgment and justice seize you.
  Beware lest wrath entice you into scoffing;
    and let not the greatness of the ransom turn you aside.
Will your cry avail to keep you from distress,
    or all the force of your strength?

Do not long for the night,
    when peoples are cut off in their place.
Take heed, do not turn to iniquity,
    for this you have chosen rather than affliction.
    Behold, God is exalted in his power;
    who is a teacher like him?
Who has prescribed for him his way,
    or who can say, 'Thou hast done wrong'?

"Remember to extol his work,
    of which men have sung.
    All men have looked on it;
    man beholds it from afar.
Behold, God is great, and we know him not;
    the number of his years is unsearchable.
    For he draws up the drops of water,
    he distils his mist in rain
which the skies pour down,
    and drop upon man abundantly.
    Can any one understand the spreading of the clouds,
    the thunderings of his pavilion?
Behold, he scatters his lightning about him,
    and covers the roots of the sea.
    For by these he judges peoples;
    he gives food in abundance.
He covers his hands with the lightning,
    and commands it to strike the mark.
    Its crashing declares concerning him,
    who is jealous with anger against iniquity.

Chapter 37

"At this also my heart trembles,
    and leaps out of its place.
    Hearken to the thunder of his voice
        and the rumbling that comes from his mouth.
Under the whole heaven he lets it go,
    and his lightning to the corners of the earth.
    After it his voice roars;
        he thunders with his majestic voice
        and he does not restrain the lightnings
        when his voice is heard.
God thunders wondrously with his voice;
    he does great things which we cannot comprehend.
    For to the snow he says, 'Fall on the earth';
        and to the shower and the rain, 'Be strong.'
He seals up the hand of every man,
    that all men may know his work.
    Then the beasts go into their lairs,
        and remain in their dens.
From its chamber comes the whirlwind,
    and cold from the scattering winds.
    By the breath of God ice is given,
        and the broad waters are frozen fast.
He loads the thick cloud with moisture;
    the clouds scatter his lightning.
    They turn round and round by his guidance,
        to accomplish all that he commands them
        on the face of the habitable world.
Whether for correction, or for his land, or for love,
    he causes it to happen.

"Hear this, O Job;
>stop and consider the wondrous works of God.
>Do you know how God lays his command upon them,
>>and causes the lightning of his cloud to shine?
>Do you know the balancings of the clouds,
>>the wondrous works of him who is perfect in knowledge,
>you whose garments are hot
>>when the earth is still because of the south wind?
>Can you, like him, spread out the skies,
>>hard as a molten mirror?
>Teach us what we shall say to him;
>>we cannot draw up our case because of darkness.
>Shall it be told him that I would speak?
>>Did a man ever wish that he would be swallowed up?

"And now men cannot look on the light
>>when it is bright in the skies,
>>when the wind has passed and cleared them.
>Out of the north comes golden splendor;
>>God is clothed with terrible majesty.
>The Almighty—we cannot find him;
>>he is great in power and justice,
>>and abundant righteousness he will not violate.
>Therefore men fear him;
>>he does not regard any who are wise in their own conceit."

Chapter 38

Then the Lord answered Job out of the whirlwind:

"Who is this that darkens counsel by words without knowledge?
  Gird up your loins like a man,
    I will question you, and you shall declare to me.

"Where were you when I laid the foundation of the earth?
    Tell me, if you have understanding.
  Who determined its measurements—surely you know!
    Or who stretched the line upon it?
On what were its bases sunk,
    or who laid its cornerstone,
  when the morning stars sang together,
    and all the sons of God shouted for joy?

"Or who shut in the sea with doors,
    when it burst forth from the womb;
  when I made the clouds its garment,
    and thick darkness its swaddling band;
and prescribed bounds for it,
    and set bars and doors,
  and said, 'Thus far shall you come, and no farther,
    and here shall your proud waves be stayed'?

"Have you commanded the morning since your days began,
    and caused the dawn to know its place,
  that it might take hold of the skirts of the earth,
    and the wicked be shaken out of it?
It is changed like clay under the seal,
    and it is dyed like a garment.

From the wicked their light is withheld,
    and their uplifted arm is broken.

"Have you entered into the springs of the sea,
    or walked in the recesses of the deep?
Have the gates of death been revealed to you,
    or have you seen the gates of deep darkness?
Have you comprehended the expanse of the earth?
    Declare, if you know all this.

"Where is the way to the dwelling of light,
    and where is the place of darkness,
  that you may take it to its territory
    and that you may discern the paths to its home?
You know, for you were born then,
    and the number of your days is great!

"Have you entered the storehouses of the snow,
    or have you seen the storehouses of the hail,
  which I have reserved for the time of trouble,
    for the day of battle and war?
What is the way to the place where the light is distributed,
    or where the east wind is scattered upon the earth?

"Who has cleft a channel for the torrents of rain,
    and a way for the thunderbolt,
  to bring rain on a land where no man is,
    on the desert in which there is no man;
to satisfy the waste and desolate land,
    and to make the ground put forth grass?

"Has the rain a father,
     or who has begotten the drops of dew?
   From whose womb did the ice come forth,
      and who has given birth to the hoarfrost of heaven?
The waters become hard like stone,
      and the face of the deep is frozen.

"Can you bind the chains of the Pleiades,
      or loose the cords of Orion?
   Can you lead forth the Mazzaroth in their season,
or can you guide the Bear with its children?
   Do you know the ordinances of the heavens?
      Can you establish their rule on the earth?

"Can you lift up your voice to the clouds,
      that a flood of waters may cover you?
   Can you send forth lightnings, that they may go,
      and say to you, 'Here we are'?
Who has put wisdom in the clouds,
      or given understanding to the mists?
   Who can number the clouds by wisdom?
      Or who can tilt the waterskins of the heavens,
when the dust runs into a mass
      and the clods cleave fast together?

"Can you hunt the prey for the lion,
      or satisfy the appetite of the young lions,
   when they crouch in their dens,
      or lie in wait in their covert?
Who provides for the raven its prey,
      when its young ones cry to God,
      and wander about for lack of food?

Chapter 39

"Do you know when the mountain goats bring forth?
Do you observe the calving of the hinds?
Can you number the months that they fulfil,
and do you know the time when they bring forth,
when they crouch, bring forth their offspring,
and are delivered of their young?
Their young ones become strong,
they grow up in the open;
they go forth, and do not return to them.

"Who has let the wild ass go free?
Who has loosed the bonds of the swift ass,
to whom I have given the steppe for his home,
and the salt land for his dwelling place?
He scorns the tumult of the city;
he hears not the shouts of the driver.
He ranges the mountains as his pasture,
and he searches after every green thing.

"Is the wild ox willing to serve you?
Will he spend the night at your crib?
Can you bind him in the furrow with ropes,
or will he harrow the valleys after you?
Will you depend on him because his strength is great,
and will you leave to him your labor?
Do you have faith in him that he will return,
and bring your grain to your threshing floor?

"The wings of the ostrich wave proudly;
but are they the pinions and plumage of love?

For she leaves her eggs to the earth,
  and lets them be warmed on the ground,
forgetting that a foot may crush them,
  and that the wild beast may trample them.
  She deals cruelly with her young, as if they were not hers;
  though her labor be in vain, yet she has no fear;
because God has made her forget wisdom,
  and given her no share in understanding.
  When she rouses herself to flee,
  she laughs at the horse and his rider.

"Do you give the horse his might?
  Do you clothe his neck with strength?
  Do you make him leap like the locust?
  His majestic snorting is terrible.
He paws in the valley, and exults in his strength;
  he goes out to meet the weapons.
  He laughs at fear, and is not dismayed;
  he does not turn back from the sword.
Upon him rattle the quiver,
  the flashing spear and the javelin.
  With fierceness and rage he swallows the ground;
  he cannot stand still at the sound of the trumpet.
When the trumpet sounds, he says 'Aha!'
  He smells the battle from afar,
  the thunder of the captains, and the shouting.

"Is it by your wisdom that the hawk soars,
  and spreads his wings toward the south?
  Is it at your command that the eagle mounts up
  and makes his nest on high?
On the rock he dwells and makes his home

in the fastness of the rocky crag.
Thence he spies out the prey;
his eyes behold it afar off.
His young ones suck up blood;
and where the slain are, there is he."

Chapter 40

And the Lord said to Job:

"Shall a faultfinder contend with the Almighty?
He who argues with God, let him answer it."

Then Job answered the Lord:

"Behold, I am of small account; what shall I answer thee?
I lay my hand upon my mouth.
I have spoken once, and I will not answer;
twice, but I will proceed no further."

Then the Lord answered Job out of the whirlwind:

"Gird up your loins like a man;
I will question you, and you declare to me.
Will you even put me in the wrong?
Will you condemn me that you may be justified?
Have you an arm like God,
and can you thunder with a voice like his?

"Deck yourself with majesty and dignity;
clothe yourself with glory and splendor.

Pour forth the overflowings of your anger,
    and look on every one that is proud, and abase him.
Look on every one that is proud, and bring him low;
    and tread down the wicked where they stand.
  Hide them all in the dust together;
    bind their faces in the world below.
Then will I also acknowledge to you,
    that your own right hand can give you victory.

"Behold, Behemoth,
    which I made as I made you;
    he eats grass like an ox.
  Behold, his strength in his loins,
    and his power in the muscles of his belly.
He makes his tail stiff like a cedar;
    the sinews of his thighs are knit together.
  His bones are tubes of bronze,
    his limbs like bars of iron.

"He is the first of the works of God;
    let him who made him bring near his sword!
  For the mountains yield food for him
    where all the wild beasts play.
Under the lotus plant he lies,
    in the covert of the reeds and in the marsh.
  For his shade the lotus tree covers him;
    the willows of the brook surround him.
Behold, if the river is turbulent he is not frightened;
    he is confident though Jordan rushes against his mouth.
  Can one take him with hooks,
    or pierce his nose with a snare?

Chapter 41

"Can you draw out Leviathan with a fishhook,
    or press down his tongue with a cord?
  Can you put a rope in his nose,
    or pierce his jaw with a hook?
Will he make many supplications to you?
    Will he speak to you soft words?
  Will he make a covenant with you
    to take him for your servant forever?
Will you play with him as with a bird,
    or will you put him on a leash for your maidens?
  Will traders bargain over him?
    Will they divide him up among the merchants?
Can you fill his skin with harpoons,
    or his head with fishing spears?
  Lay hands on him;
    think of the battle; you will not do it again!
Behold, the hope of a man is disappointed;
    he is laid low even at the sight of him.
  No one is so fierce that he dares to stir him up.
    Who then is he that can stand before me?
Who has given to me, that I should repay him?
    Whatever is under the whole heaven is mine.

"I will not keep silence concerning his limbs,
    or his mighty strength, or his goodly frame.
  Who can strip off his outer garment?
    Who can penetrate his double coat of mail?
Who can open the doors of his face?
    Round about his teeth is terror.

His back is made of rows of shields,
  shut up closely as with a seal.
One is so near to another
  that no air can come between them.
  They are joined to one another;
    they clasp each other and cannot be separated.
His sneezings flash forth light,
  and his eyes are like the eyelids of the dawn.
  Out of his mouth go flaming torches;
    sparks of fire leap forth.
Out of his nostrils comes forth smoke,
  as from a boiling pot and burning rushes.
  His breath kindles coals,
    and a flame comes forth from his mouth.
In his neck abides strength,
  and terror dances before him.
  The folds of his flesh cleave together,
    firmly cast upon him and immovable.
His heart is hard as a stone,
  hard as the nether millstone.
  When he rises himself up the mighty are afraid;
    at the crashing they are beside themselves.
Though the sword reaches him, it does not avail;
  nor the spear, the dart, or the javelin.
  He counts iron as straw, and bronze as rotten wood.
The arrow cannot make him flee;
  for him the slingstones are turned to stubble.
  Clubs are counted as stubble;
    he laughs at the rattle of javelins.
His underparts are like sharp potsherds;
  he spreads himself like a threshing sledge on the mire.

He makes the deep boil like a pot;
    he makes the sea like a pot of ointment.
Behind him he leaves a shining wake;
    one would think the deep to be hoary.
Upon earth there is not his like,
    a creature without fear.
He beholds everything that is high;
    he is king over all the sons of pride."

Chapter 42

Then Job answered the Lord:

"I know that thou canst do all things,
    and that no purpose of thine can be thwarted.
'Who is this that hides counsel without knowledge?'
Therefore I have uttered what I did not understand,
    things too wonderful for me, which I did not know.
'Hear, and I will speak;
    I will question you, and you declare to me.'
I had heard of thee by the hearing of the ear,
    but now my eye sees thee;
therefore I despise myself,
    and repent in dust and ashes."

After the Lord had spoken these words to Job, the Lord said to Eliphaz the Temanite: "My wrath is kindled against you and against your two friends; for you have not spoken of me what is right, as my servant Job has. Now therefore take seven bulls and seven rams, and go to my servant Job, and offer up for yourselves a burnt offering; and my servant Job shall pray for you, for I will accept his prayer not to deal with you according to your folly; for you have not spoken of me what is right, as my servant Job has." So Eliphaz the Temanite and Bildad the Shuhite and Zophar the Naamathite went and did what the Lord had told them; and the Lord accepted Job's prayer.

And the Lord restored the fortunes of Job, when he had prayed for his friends; and the Lord gave Job twice as much as he had before. Then came to him all his brothers and sisters and all who had known him before, and ate bread with him in his house; and they showed him sympathy and comforted him for all the evil that the Lord had brought upon him; and each of them gave him a piece of money and a ring of gold. And the Lord blessed the latter days of Job more than his beginning; and he had fourteen thousand sheep, six thousand camels, a thousand yoke of oxen, and a thousand she-asses. He had also seven sons and three daughters. And he called the name of the first Jemimah; and the name of the second Keziah; and the name of the third Keren-happuch. And in all the land there were no women so fair as Job's daughters; and their father gave them inheritance among their brothers. And after this Job lived a hundred and forty years, and saw his sons, and his son's sons, four generations. And Job died, an old man, and full of days.

On the intertwined subjects of Job and theodicy, a large and venerable literature exists, including rabbinic, Christian, and secular philosophical sources. And it is constantly being added to. What follows is a small but enticing selection of excerpts from this rich commentary. Some are taken from a book now sadly out of print, an excellent anthology with a first-rate bibliography called *The Dimensions of Job* (1969), edited by the late Nahum N. Glatzer, a remarkable scholar of Judaism, of Kafka, and of the philosophy of religion.

MOSES MAIMONIDES
1135–1204

The realization of God's unfathomable Providence gives man the means of ordering his own life and bearing the afflictions it may bring.

Much less can we compare the manner in which God rules and manages His creatures with the manner in which we rule and manage certain beings. We must content ourselves with this, and believe that nothing is hidden from God, as Elihu says: "for his eyes are upon the ways of man, and he seeth all his goings. There is no darkness nor shadow of death, where the workers of iniquity may hide themselves" (34:21, 22). But the term "management," when applied to God, has not the same meaning which it has when applied to us; and when we say that He rules His creatures we do not mean that He does the same as we do when we rule over other beings. The term "rule" has not the same definition in both cases; it signifies two different notions, which have nothing in common but the name. In the same manner, as there is a difference between works of nature and productions of human handicraft, so there is a difference between God's rule, providence, and intention in reference to all natural forces, and our rule, providence, and intention in reference to things which are the objects of our rule, providence, and intention. This lesson is the principal object of the whole Book of Job; it lays down this principle of faith, and recommends us to derive a proof from nature, that we should not fall into the error of imagining His knowledge to be similar to ours, or His intention, providence, and rule similar to ours. When we know this we shall find everything that may befall us easy to bear; mishap will create no doubts in our hearts concerning God, whether He knows our affairs or not, whether He provides for us or abandons us. On the contrary, our fate will increase our love of God; as is said in the end of this prophecy: "Therefore I abhor myself and repent concerning the dust of ashes" (42:6); and as our Sages say: "The pious do everything out of love, and rejoice in their own afflictions."

JOHN CALVIN
1509–1564

For man to demand a hearing of God and, worse, to argue with him at it represent the very embodiments of human arrogance. Humble obedience is the only pathway to God's court.

For is it not to pervert the order of nature, that mortal man who is nothing anticipates his Creator, and makes Him give audience, and that God meanwhile keeps silence? How far does this go? It is, nevertheless, what we do, always and whenever we shall murmur against God when we shall tear His Word in pieces, as we frame propositions at will, saying, "This is how it seems to me." What is the cause of this, unless we wish that God keep silence before us, and that we be heard above Him? Is this not a pure rage? So then, to correct this arrogance that is in us, let us learn not to presume to answer our God; knowing that when we shall come before Him, He will have the authority to examine us; indeed, according to His will, and not according to our appetite for it; and at our station; and that when He will have closed our mouth, and He will have commenced to speak, we shall be more than confounded; let us learn to humble ourselves, so that we may be taught by Him; and when we shall have been taught, may He make us contemplate His brightness in the midst of the shadows of the world. Meanwhile, let us also learn to serve Him and to adore Him in everything and by everything. For this is also how we shall have well profited in the school of God; it will be when we shall have learned to magnify Him, and to attribute to Him such a glory that we may find good, everything that proceeds from Him. Meanwhile, may we also be advised to be displeased with ourselves, in order to run to Him to find there the good that is lacking in us. And beyond that may it please Him to so govern us by His Holy Spirit that, being filled with His glory, we may have wherewith to glorify ourselves, not in us, but in Him alone.

Now we shall bow in humble reverence before the face of our God.

MARTIN BUBER
1878–1965

*Job, who suffers, attains the vision of God through his suffering. He
becomes God's witness on earth, as God is his witness in heaven.*

The creation itself already means communication between creator and creature. The just creator gives to all His creatures His
boundary, so that each may become fully itself. Designedly man is
lacking in this presentation of heaven and earth, in which man is
shown the justice that is greater than his, and is shown that he
with his justice, which intends to give to everyone what is due to
him, is called only to emulate the divine justice, which gives to
everyone what he is. In the face of such divine teaching as this, it
would be indeed impossible for the sufferer to do aught else than
put "his hand upon his mouth" (40:4), and to confess (42:3) that he
had erred in speaking of things inconceivable to him. And nothing else could have come of it except this recognition—if he had
heard only a voice "from the whirlwind" (38:1; 40:6). But the voice
is the voice of *Him who answers,* the voice of Him that "heard"
(31:35), and appeared so as to be "found" by him (23:3). In vain
Job had tried to penetrate to God through the divine remoteness;
now God draws near to him. No more does God hide Himself—
only the storm cloud of His sublimity still shrouds Him—and
Job's eye "sees" Him (42:5). The absolute power is for human personality's sake become personality. God offers Himself to the sufferer who, in the depth of his despair, keeps to God with his
refractory complaint; He offers Himself to him as an answer. It is
true, "the overcoming of the riddle of suffering can only come
from the domain of revelation," but it is not the revelation in
general that is here decisive, but the particular revelation to the
individual: the revelation as an *answer* to the individual sufferer

concerning the question of his suffering, the self-limitation of
God to a person, answering a person.

The *way* of this poem leads from the first view to the fourth.
The God of the first view, the God of the legend borrowed by the
poet, works on the basis of "enticement"; the second, the God of
friends, works on the basis of purposes apparent to us, purposes of
punishment or, especially in the speeches of Elihu (which are
probably a later addition), of purification and education; the
third, the God of the protesting Job, works against every reason
and purpose; and the fourth, the God of revelation, works from
His godhead, in which every reason and purpose held by man is
at once abolished and fulfilled. It is clear that this God, who
answers from the whirlwind, is different from the God of the
prologue; the declaration about the secret of divine action would
be turned into a mockery if the fact of that "wager" were put over
against it. But even the speeches of the friends and of Job cannot
be harmonized with it. Presumably the poet, who frequently
shows himself to be a master of irony, left the prologue, which
seems completely opposed to his intention, unchanged in content
in order to establish the foundation for the multiplicity of views
that follows. But in truth the view of the prologue is meant to be
ironical and unreal; the view of the friends is only logically "true"
and demonstrates to us that man must not subject God to the rules
of logic. Job's view is real, and therefore, so to speak, the negative
of truth; and the view of the voice speaking from the whirlwind
is the supralogical truth of reality. God justifies Job: he has spoken
"rightly" (42:7), unlike the friends. And as the poet often uses
words of the prologue as motive words in different senses, so also
here he makes God call Job as there by the name of His "servant,"
and repeat it by way of emphasis four times. Here this epithet
appears in its true light. Job, the faithful rebel, like Abraham,
Moses, David, and Isaiah, stands in the succession of men so des-

ignated by God, a succession that leads to Deutero-Isaiah's "servant of YHVH," whose suffering especially links him with Job.

"And my servant Job shall pray for you"—with these words God sends the friends home (42:8). It is the same phrase as that in which YHVH in the story of Abraham (Gen. 20:7) certifies the patriarch, that he is His *navi*. It will be found that in all the pre-exilic passages, in which the word is used in the sense of intercession (and this apparently was its first meaning), it is only used of men called prophets. The significance of Job's intercession is emphasized by the epilogue (which, apart from the matter of the prayer, the poet apparently left as it was), in that the turning point in Job's history, the "restoration" (Job 42:10) and first of all his healing, begins the moment he prays "for his friends." This saying is the last of the reminiscences of prophetic life and language found in this book. As if to stress this connection, Job's first complaint begins (3:3 ff.) with the cursing of his birth, reminding us of Jeremiah's words (Jer. 20:14), and the first utterance of the friends is poured out in figures of speech taken from the prophetic world (Job 4:12 ff.), the last of which (4:16) modifies the peculiar form of revelation of Elijah's story (I Kings 19:12). Job's recollection of divine intimacy, of "the converse of God upon his tent" (Job 29:4), is expressed in language derived from Jeremiah (Jer. 23:18, 22), and his quest, which reaches fulfillment, to "see" God, touches the prophetic experience which only on Mount Sinai were non-prophets allowed to share (Exod. 24:10, 17). Jeremiah's historical figure, that of the suffering prophet, apparently inspired the poet to compose his poem of the man of suffering, who by his suffering attained the vision of God, and in all his revolt was God's witness on earth (cf. Isa. 43:12; 44:8), as God was his witness in heaven.

YEHEZKEL KAUFMANN
1889–1963

God's ultimate revelation, his ultimate grace to us, is his manifestation
of himself. All human wisdom is transcended by this supreme act
of providence.

Is the whole answer, then, that God's ways are hidden from man?
Surely the poet desired to say more. It is noteworthy that in these
final chapters wisdom and legendary elements commingle. God's
words are sapiential, but their framework is a legend: God speaks
in a daytime theophany out of the storm. Is this not the embodi-
ment in legend of wisdom's maxim "He has said to man: Behold,
the fear of the Lord, that is wisdom" (28:28)? In the theophany
and discourse with man, God's ultimate grace shines forth, the
grace of revelation. This is His supreme favor. Not what He said,
but His very manifestation is the last, decisive argument. "I had
heard of Thee only a report, but now my eye beholds Thee, therefore I despise myself and repent in dust and ashes." These are
Job's last words (42:5 f.). If the almighty God has consented to
reveal Himself to mortal man and instruct him, what further
room is there to question His providence and His concern for the
world?

God's answer is the beginning of Job's restoration. In itself,
it restored his last and severest loss, his faith in God's providence. God's reproach of the companions next restores his honor
and good repute, which were lost consequent to his afflictions.
Lastly, God restores his material possessions which were the first
to perish.

The answer of the book of Job is, then, religious to its very core.
It comes from the realm of revelation, not wisdom; this is the dis-
tinctive Israelite feature of the book. A tragic conflict broke out

between the righteous man and sage in Job, The righteous man
believed in the existence of God; the sage does not argue with this
belief, but seeks to separate God from the idea of morality and
justice. God exists, but His rule is not moral. This separation is
rejected by the book; the idea of God necessarily includes the
moral idea. The Israelite sage contends with God, but in the end,
he, like the righteous man, "lives by faith" (Hab. 2:4).

LEON ROTH
1896–1963

*Job is vindicated by his trust in God even when he is brought to the
brink of extinction. God can be found no matter where we are, and
no matter where we are, God can find us.*

As in Jonah, the ultimate secret is seen to lie in the fact of creation.
But creation now outsteps not only humankind; it outsteps the
sentient world too. It covers the mountain goats and the eagles,
the war horse and the ostrich, but also and primarily the sea and
the stars, the winds and the frost and the hail. Its rain falls to satisfy the waste and desolate ground and to cause the tender grass to
spring forth. The greensward too is the work of God; so is the
desert where there is no man.

The instructive thing is that Job declares himself convinced.
He is silenced and lays his hand upon his mouth: "I had heard of
Thee before but by the hearing of the ear; but now mine eye seeth
Thee" (42:5). It is often asked what he became convinced by, and
what it is that he became convinced of; but the answer is surely
that whereas there had been *brought before* him the wonders of
the creation, what he *saw* was the far greater wonder, the wonder
of the creator. He does *not* say: "Mine eye seeth behemoth and
leviathan." He says: "Mine eye seeth *Thee.*" He had an immediate

apprehension of the unity that lies behind the variety and majesty of the world, the unity in which power, authority, goodness, and wisdom meet together in cosmic creativity. Job was justly proud of his integrity. He had seen God as his enemy. He had challenged God to justify His rule of the world. God retorts by showing Job that the world is an even stranger affair than Job had imagined, but strange as it is, it yet has meaning.

Jonah, like Jeremiah, was a prophet to the world at large. Job is man as such. Jonah says he serves the God of heaven and earth who created the seas and dry land, and he is made to live up to his profession. Job demonstrates, to the incredulity of the powers of heaven itself, that it is not external circumstance that makes a man. Neither Jonah nor Job, the lesson of the whale and of the whirlwind, is, as has been so often imagined, primitive or naive. They are both works of advanced reflection. They are master-pieces of irony, and irony springs from a body of settled opinion so deeply embedded in the popular mind as to serve as a permanent background for thought. Irony dares to suggest that received opinion, however deeply embedded and widely spread, may be wrong.

The book of Job turns on the question of the nature of religion: can man serve God for nought? The test is made *in corpore vili* ["on an ordinary body"]. Job is put on the operating table and examined. When Job says, "Though He slay me, yet will I trust in Him" (13:15), he vindicates both himself and God.

The book of Jonah depicts the bearers of God's oracles: their recalcitrance, their suffering, their doubts. They flee, or are made to flee, from country to country, yet they cannot escape the Word.

As God is found everywhere, so man can live anywhere. He can survive even the inside of a whale. And just as God can put man there, so from there can man seek for God, and so too can God find man.

MARGARETE SUSMAN
1874–1966

*Even in the overwhelming vastness of God's silence in the face of
human anguish, he is made present by man's cry to him.*

Job, who in his suffering was delivered by God to his tempter,
prefigures in his fate the sorrowful fate of the Jewish people in
exile. . . .

Acting therefore on the belief that they have done everything
for their God, Israel, like Job, unceasingly asks for the connection
between human suffering and guilt, which is as much as saying
they ask for divine justice. The very fact that they suffer, and suffer for reasons unknown, forces the Jews in exile to a theodicy;
that is to say, it imposes upon them again and again the attempt to
justify God and to explain suffering and guilt and their connection. There is not one great achievement of Judaism in exile that
at bottom is not a theodicy.

Since the ghettos have been dissolved, the Jews have come to
share without mediation the fate of the occidental world, and
their homelessness . . . has received its final completing portion of
isolation. God, for whose sake they have accepted all this, cannot
be found any longer, because for the occidental world—of which
the Jew is now an integral part—the revealed God whom the Jew
has accepted has become, in a manner unimaginable till now, the
Deus absconditus, the absent God, the God who simply can no
longer be found. . . . But when the Jew has lost his God, he has
lost everything. The reverse of Abraham's unconditional sacrifi-
cial readiness is the absolute desolation of the Jew when God
abandons him.

Thus, the isolation and the abandonment of the Jew in exile

has been completed with his assimilation into the occidental world. But the dispute with God cannot cease even now. The Jew cannot remain silent when God hides Himself now as He hid Himself before Job. Because, just as He evaded Job in his personal fate, so He evades the modern Jew in his universal fate. For this reason the process against God must assume a new shape; it must start anew and in a new version: a version in which God is all silence and man alone speaks. And yet, though His name is never mentioned, only He is addressed.

H. H. ROWLEY
1890–1969

Job was honored by God for by his very suffering he served him.
In his fellowship with God, occasioned by his suffering,
Job was far more blessed than the most prosperous
among the wicked.

The problem of suffering is as real a problem today as it was in the days of our author, and Christian theology is as impotent as Jewish to solve it. It is sometimes thought that the faith that beyond this life there is another, where the injustices and inequalities of this life may be rectified, offers an answer to the problem. In truth it offers none. When the wicked is seen to prosper, it may be possible to find some comfort in the thought of what lies before him in the next world—though this is not a very exalted comfort . . . this can offer no possible explanation of his present sufferings. The book of Job is far more profound in its message that here and now the pious sufferer has no reason to envy the prosperous wicked. The wicked may have his prosperity, but the pious may have God; and in God he has far more than the other. The inequalities of life belong to man's outer lot; but this is immaterial to his spiritual life.

HORACE M. KALLEN
1882–1974

It is not prosperity that measures the value of human existence but, rather, the inward character of integrity maintained against all odds.

. . . the ultimate value of human existence is not existence merely; the ultimate value of human existence is the quality and distinction of existence of which consists a man's character, his nature as this or that kind of man. "Behold," declares Job, "I know that He will slay me; I have no hope. Nevertheless will I maintain my ways before Him" (13:15). "Till I die will I not put away mine integrity from me; my righteousness hold I fast, and will not let it go. My heart shall not reproach me so long as I live" (27:5 f.).

To cling to his integrity while he lives, to assert and to realize the excellences appropriate to his nature as a man, as this particular kind of man, knowing all the while that this is to be accomplished in a world which was not made for him, in which he shares his claim on the consideration of Omnipotence with the infinitude of its creatures that alike manifest its powers—this is the destiny of man. He must take his chance in a world that doesn't care about him any more than about anything else. He must maintain his ways with courage rather than with faith, with self-respect rather than with humility or better perhaps, with a faith that is courage, a humility that is self-respect. When ultimately confronted with the inward character of Omnipotence, man realizes that, on its part alone, moral indifference can be genuine justice. Its providence, its indifference, its justice—they are all one. Otherwise nothing else but the favored, the chosen creature could exist. Hence, when Yahweh reveals Himself to Job as the creative providence sustaining even the most impotent of living things and destroying even the strongest, Job realizes that not prosperity but excellence is the justification of human life, and the very indifference of Yahweh comforts him. "I know" he declares,

> that Thou canst do all things,
> And that no purpose of Thine can be restrained.
> By hearsay only had I heard of Thee,
> But now mine eyes seeth Thee,
> Wherefore I recant my challenge, and am comforted
> Amid dust and ashes.   (42:2–6)

. . . Such is the theory of life in which the ripest wisdom of the Hebraic tradition found expression. Its beginnings are strong in Jeremiah, its growth is a function of the progressive postponement of Yahweh's promised Golden Age, of the irony of a chosen people that suffers, of individual tragedies like Jeremiah's and Zerubbabel's. In it the soul of man comes to itself and is freed. It is a humanism terrible and unique. For, unlike the Greek humanism it does not enfranchise the mind by interpreting the world in terms of its own substance, by declaring an ultimate happy destiny for man in a world immortally in harmony with his nature and needs; it is not an anthropomorphosis, not a pathetic fallacy. It is without illusion concerning the quality, extent, and possibilities of the life of man, without illusion concerning his relation to God. It accepts them, and makes of the human soul the citadel of man—even against Omnipotence itself—wherein he cherishes his integrity, and, so cherishing, is victorious in the warfare of living even when life is lost.

PAUL WEISS

1901–

If the just suffer while the wicked appear to prosper, why be just? The just man enhances his own goodness and that of others while wicked men defeat themselves ultimately by depriving themselves of the complete humanity given only by goodness.

There are at least ten different kinds of evil, though philosophers have been inclined to mention only three. Since there are no well-turned designations and definitions for most of them, we must make up a set as we go along. With some warrant in tradition, we can perhaps designate the different kinds of evil as *sin, bad intention, wickedness, guilt, vice, physical suffering, psychological suffering, social suffering, natural evil, and metaphysical evil.* . . .

God has His own standards of goodness and does not disturb the natural order of things. If "providence" be understood to refer to an irresistible divine force supporting what men take to be good, there is then no providence. But God could offer material which the universe might utilize in its own way, and God could preserve whatever goods the universe throws up on the shores of time. If He did, He would exhibit a providential concern for the universe and its inhabitants, but one that does not conflict with the brutal fact that there are both human and natural evils.

No one of the foregoing nine forms of evil is necessary. It is conceivable that none of them might be. To be sure, wherever there are men, there is the evil of guilt; but men need not exist. To be sure, if we have a universe of interplaying things, there will be destructive natural forces, but the universe might conceivably reach a stage of equilibrium. Each atom might vibrate in place and interfere with nothing beyond. What could not be avoided by the things in any universe whatsoever is the tenth kind of evil, *metaphysical* evil, the evil of being one among many, of possessing only a fragment of reality, of lacking the reality and thus the power and good possessed by all the others.

Any universe whatsoever, created or uncreated, is one in which each part is less than perfect precisely because it is other than the rest, and is deprived therefore of the reality the rest contain. God might have made, could He make anything at all, a better universe than this, for He could have eliminated or muted some of the forms of evil that now prevail. But He could not have made this universe in detail or as a whole completely free of all defect. No matter how good and concerned God might be, and no matter how few of the other nine types of evil happen to exist, there is always metaphysical evil to mark the fact that the universe is not God and God not the universe.

Much of the foregoing can be summarized in four questions and answers:

Why do bad men prosper? They do not.
Why does God not make bad men suffer more than they do? He does not interfere with the workings of the universe on the whole or in detail.
Why do good men suffer? Suffering and goodness have quite dissimilar causes.
Is God on the side of the right? God has His own standards. But to be religious is to have a faith that His standards will eventually be ours.

HAYIM GREENBERG
1889–1953

The person who would believe in God must cease looking for confir-
mations which he can grasp with his reason and touch with his hands.
This is to be religious, for God's logic is beyond human reason.

Religious thought must, once and for all, renounce rationalist interpretation and justification of the ways of God. There exists no science of God, and no way of studying His ways. And whoever seeks a sign of God's justice and goodness in the events of the world, an empirical and demonstrable confirmation that He exists and that He is the bearer of the highest good, will never find it; and if one claims that he has found such confirmation, this is conscious or unconscious falsehood. If one is to be honest with oneself, one must either deny the existence of God or come to the conclusion reached by the hero of the Latin drama *Thyestes:* "I have always maintained and I will continue to maintain that the gods exist in heaven but that they take no interest in the doings of mankind. Were they to take an interest, then the good would flourish and the evil would suffer." This is the only possible conclusion if one is to retain a rationalist conception of the world. Religious man, on the other hand, must learn from Job to believe without understanding, to trust without explanations.

Job was comforted when he sat in dust and ashes. Who comforted him? Not his friends with their theological scholarship, not even God Himself. God's voice from the storm explained nothing to Job—it merely expanded the area of his not knowing and not understanding; it opened before him unlimited horizons of the inconceivable and impenetrable, and deepened the mystery of existence. Job was consoled by the realization that his suffering was a drop in the endless mystery of being and living.

The true believer practices the most heroic defiance in the world. His logic may be most strange and paradoxical, as in the case of Job, who declared, "Even though He slay me, yet will I believe in Him" (13:15). Those who regard such an attitude as absurd cannot be proved wrong, but people who reason thus have nothing to do with religion.

RUDOLF OTTO
1869–1937

Job attains peace in the manifestation of the absolute wondrousness of God's revealed magnificence.

In the thirty-eighth chapter of Job we have the element of the mysterious displayed in rare purity and completeness, and this chapter may well rank among the most remarkable in the history of religion. Job has been reasoning with his friends against Elohim [God], and—as far as concerns them—he has been obviously in the right. They are compelled to be dumb before him. And then Elohim Himself appears to conduct His own defense in person. And He conducts it to such effect that Job avows himself to be overpowered—truly and rightly overpowered—not merely silenced by superior strength. Then he confesses: "Therefore I abhor myself and repent in dust and ashes" (42:6). That is an admission of inward convincement and conviction, not of impotent collapse and submission to merely superior power. Nor is there here at all the frame of mind to which St. Paul now and then gives utterance; e.g., "Shall the thing formed say to Him that formed it, Why hast Thou made me thus? Hath not the potter power over the clay, of the same lump to make one vessel unto honor, and another unto dishonor?" (Rom. 9:20, 21). To interpret the passage in Job thus would be a misunderstanding of it. This chapter does not proclaim, as Paul does, the renunciation of, the realization of the impossibility of, a "theodicy"; rather, it aims at putting forward a real theodicy of its own, and a better one than that of Job's friends—a theodicy able to convince even a Job, and not only to convince him, but utterly to still every inward doubt that assailed his soul. For latent in the weird experience that Job underwent in the revelation of Elohim is at once an inward relaxing of his soul's anguish and an appeasement, an appeasement that would alone and in itself perfectly suffice as the solution of the problem of the book of Job, even without Job's rehabilitation in chapter 42, which is merely a later addition to the real narrative. But what is this strange "moment" of experience that operates at once as a vindication of God to Job and a reconciliation of Job to God?

In the words put into the mouth of Elohim, nearly every note is sounded that the situation may prepare one to expect a priori: the summons to Job, and the demonstration of God's overwhelming power, His sublimity and greatness, and His surpassing wisdom. This last would yield forthwith a plausible and rational solution of the whole problem, if only the argument were here completed with some such sentences as: "My ways are higher than your ways; in my deeds and my actions I have ends that you understand not," viz., the testing or purification of the godly man, or ends that concern the whole universe as such, into which the single man must fit himself with all his sufferings.

If you start from rational ideas and concepts, you absolutely thirst for such a conclusion to the discourse. But nothing of the kind follows; nor does the chapter intend at all to suggest such teleological reflections or solutions. In the last resort it relies on something quite different from anything that can be exhaustively rendered in rational concepts, namely, on the sheer absolute wondrousness that transcends thought, on the mysterium, presented

in its pure, non-rational form. All the glorious examples from nature speak very plainly in this sense. The eagle, that "dwelleth and abideth on the rock, upon the crag of the rock, and the strong place," whose "eyes behold afar off" her prey, and whose "young ones also suck up blood, and where the slain are, there is she" (39:27–30)—this eagle is in truth no evidence for the teleological wisdom that "prepares all cunningly and well," but is rather the creature of strangeness and marvel, in whom the wondrousness of its creator becomes apparent. And the same is true of the ostrich with its inexplicable instincts. The ostrich is indeed, as here depicted and "rationally" considered, a crucial difficulty rather than an evidence of wisdom, and it affords singularly little help if we are seeking purpose in nature: "For she leaveth her eggs in the earth, and warmeth them in the dust, and forgetteth that the foot may crush them or that the wild beast may break them. She is hardened against her young ones, as though they were not hers; her labor is in vain without fear; because God hath deprived her of wisdom, neither hath He imparted to her under-standing" (39:14–17).

It is the same with the wild ass (39:5) and the wild ox (39:9). These are beasts whose complete "dysteleology" or negation of purposiveness is truly magnificently depicted; but, nevertheless, with their mysterious instincts and the riddle of their genera-tion, this very negation of purpose becomes a thing of baffling sig-nificance, as in the case of the wild goat (39:1) and the hind. The "wisdom" of the inward parts (38:36), and the "knowledge" of Dayspring, winds, and clouds, with the mysterious ways in which they come and go, arise and vanish, shift and veer and re-form; and the wonderful Pleiades aloft in heaven, with Orion and "Arc-turus and his sons"—these serve but to emphasize the same les-son. It is conjectured that the descriptions of the hippopotamus (*behemoth*) and crocodile (*leviathan*) (in 40:15 ff.) are a later inter-

polation. This may well be the fact; but, if so, it must be admitted that the interpolator has felt the point of the entire section extraordinarily well. He only brings to its grossest expression the thought intended by all the other examples of animals; they gave portents only, he gives us "monsters"—but "the monstrous" is just the "mysterious" in a gross form. Assuredly these beasts would be the most unfortunate examples that one could hit upon if searching for evidences of the purposefulness of the divine "wisdom." But they, no less than all the previous examples and the whole context, tenor, and sense of the entire passage, do express in masterly fashion the downright stupendousness, the well-nigh demonic and wholly incomprehensible character of the eternal creative power; how, incalculable and "wholly other," it mocks at all conceiving but can yet stir the mind to its depths, fascinate and overbrim the heart. What is meant is the mysterium not as mysterious simply, but at the same time also as "fascinating" and "august"; and here, too, these latter meanings live, not in any explicit concepts, but in the tone, the enthusiasm, in the very rhythm of the entire exposition. And here is indeed the point of the whole passage, comprising alike the theodicy and the appeasement and calming of Job's soul. The mysterium, simply as such, would merely (as discussed above) be a part of the "absolute inconceivability" of the *numen,* and that, though it might strike Job utterly dumb, could not convince him inwardly. That of which we are conscious is rather an intrinsic value in the incomprehensible—a value inexpressible, positive, and "fascinating." This is incommensurable with thoughts of rational human teleology and is not assimilated to them: it remains in all its mystery. But it is as it becomes felt in consciousness that Elohim is justified and at the same time Job's soul brought to peace.

WILLIAM BARRETT
1913–

As flesh and blood a human being is bound to the earth. Man knows God as his creator and must trust him to somehow raise him from the dust of mortality.

The relation between Job and God is on the level of existence and not of reason. Rational doubt, in the sense of the term that the later philosophic tradition of the West has made familiar to us, never enters Job's mind, even in the very paroxysm of his revolt. His relation to God remains one of faith from start to finish, though, to be sure, his faith takes on the varying shapes of revolt, anger, dismay, and confusion. Job says, *"Though He slay me, yet will I trust in Him"* (13:15), but he adds what is usually not brought to our attention as emphatically as the first part of his saying: *"But I will maintain my own ways before Him."* Job retains his own identity (his "own ways") in confronting the creator, before whom he is as nothing. Job in the many shades and turnings of faith is close to those primitive peoples who may break, revile, and spit upon the image of a god who is no longer favorable. Similarly, in Psalm 89 David rebukes Yahweh for all the tribulations that He has poured upon His people, and there can be no doubt that we are here at the stage in history where faith is so real that it permits man to call God to account. It is a stage close to the primitive, but also a considerable step beyond it: for the Hebrew had added a new element, faith, and so internalized what was simply the primitive's anger against his god. When faith is full, it dares to express its anger, for faith is the openness of the whole man toward his God, and therefore must be able to encompass all human modes of being. . . .

Faith as a concrete mode of being of the human person precedes faith as the intellectual assent to a proposition, just as truth as a concrete mode of human being precedes the truth of any proposition. Moreover, this trust that embraces a man's anger and dismay, his bones and his bowels—the whole man, in short—does not yet permit any separation of soul from body, of reason from man's irrational other half. In Job and the Psalms man is very much a man of flesh and blood, and his being as a creature is described time and again in images that are starkly physical:

> Remember, I beseech Thee, that Thou hast made me as clay;
> and wilt Thou bring me into dust again?
> Hast Thou not poured me out as milk,
> and curdled me like cheese?
> Thou hast clothed me with skin and flesh,
> and hast fenced me with bones and sinews.   (10:9 ff.)

And when Psalm 22 speaks of the sense of abandonment and dereliction, it uses not the high, rarefied language of introspection but the most powerful cry of the physical:

My God, my God, why hast Thou forsaken me? . . .
Thou art He that took me out of the womb:
Thou didst make me hope when I was upon my mother's breasts.
I was cast upon Thee from the womb:
Thou art my God from my mother's belly. . . .

I am poured out like water,
and all my bones are out of joint;
my heart is like wax;
it is melted in the midst of my bowels.
My strength is dried up like a potsherd;
.and my tongue cleaveth to my jaws;
and Thou hast brought me into the dust of death.   (Ps. 22:1, 9 f., 14 f.)

... As a man of flesh and blood, biblical man was very much bound to the earth. "Remember, I beseech Thee, that Thou hast made me as clay; and wilt Thou bring me into dust again?" Bound to the dust, he was bound to death: a creature of time, whose being was temporal through and through. The idea of eternity—eternity for man—does not bulk large in the Bible beside the power and frequency of the images of man's mortality. God is the Everlasting, who, though He meets man face to face, is altogether beyond human ken and comparison; while man, who is as nothing before his creator, is like all other beings of the dust a creature of a day, whose temporal substance is repeatedly compared to wind and shadow.

> Man that is born of woman
> is of few days, and full of trouble.
> He cometh forth like a flower, and is cut down:
> he fleeth also as a shadow,
> and continueth not.   (Job 14:1 f.)

Hebraism contains no eternal realm of essences, which Greek philosophy was to fabricate, through Plato, as affording the intellectual deliverance from the evil of time. Such a realm of eternal essences is possible only for a *detached* intellect, one who, in Plato's phrase, becomes a "spectator of all time and all existence." This ideal of the philosopher as the highest human type—the theoretical intellect who, from the vantage point of eternity, can survey all time and existence—is altogether foreign to the Hebraic concept of the man of faith who is passionately committed to his own mortal being. Detachment was for the Hebrew an impermissible state of mind, a vice rather than a virtue; or rather it was something that biblical man was not yet even able to conceive, since he had not reached the level of rational abstraction of the Greek. His existence was too earth-bound, too laden with the oppressive images of mortality, to permit him to experience the philosopher's detachment. The notion of the immortality of the soul as an intellectual substance (and that that immortality might even be demonstrated rationally) had not dawned upon the mind of biblical man. If he hoped at all to escape mortality, it was on the basis of personal trust that his creator might raise him once again from the dust.

ARCHIBALD MACLEISH
1892–1982

God needed the suffering of Job to know that Job would love him in spite of everything. God depends upon man's fortitude and love.

If one were to write an argument to go at the head of the book of Job in some private notebook of one's own, it might well be written in these words: Satan, who is the denial of life, who is the kingdom of death, cannot be overcome by God who is his opposite, who is the kingdom of life, except by man's persistence in the love of God in spite of every reason to withhold his love, every suffering.

And if one were then to write an explanation of that argument, the explanation might be this: Man depends on God for all things; God depends on man for one. Without man's love, God does not exist as God, only as creator, and love is the one thing no one, not even God Himself, can command. It is a free gift or it is nothing. And it is most itself, most free, when it is offered in spite of suffering, of injustice, and of death.

And if one were to attempt, finally, to reduce this explanation and this argument to a single sentence which might stand at the end of the book to close it, the sentence might read this way: The justification of the injustice of the universe is not our blind acceptance of God's inexplicable will, nor our trust in God's love—His dark and incomprehensible love—for us, but our human love, not-withstanding anything, for Him.

Acceptance—even Dante's acceptance of God's will is not enough. Love—love of life, love of the world, love of God, love in spite of everything—is the answer, the only possible answer, to our ancient human cry against injustice.

It is for this reason that God, at the end of the poem, answers Job not in the language of justice but in the language of beauty and power and glory, signifying that it is not because He is just but because He is God that He deserves His creature's adoration.

And it is true. We do not love God because we can believe in Him; we believe in God because we can love Him. It is because we—even we—can love God that we can conceive Him, and it is because we can conceive Him that we can live. To speak of "justice" is to demand something for ourselves, to ask something of life, to require that we be treated according to our dues. But love, as Saint Paul told the Corinthians, does not "seek her own" (I Cor. 13:5). Love creates. Love creates even God, for how else have we come to Him, any of us, but through love?

Man, the scientists say, is the animal that thinks. They are wrong. Man is the animal that loves. It is in man's love that God exists and triumphs, in man's love that life is beautiful, in man's love that the world's injustice is resolved. To hold together in one thought those terrible opposites of good and evil which struggle in the world is to be capable of life, and only love will hold them so.

Our labor always, like Job's labor, is to learn through suffering to love . . . to love even that which lets us suffer.

ACKNOWLEDGMENTS

Grateful acknowledgment is made to the following for permission to reprint previously published material:

Balkin Agency, Inc.: Excerpt from *The Prophetic Faith* by Martin Buber, translated by Carlyle Witton-Davies (New York: The Macmillan Company, pp. 188–197, with a new edition forthcoming from Syracuse University Press, in 1999), copyright © 1949, copyright renewed 1976. Reprinted by permission of the Balkin Agency, Inc.

Commentary and *Paul Weiss:* Excerpt from "God, Job, and Evil" by Paul Weiss (*Commentary,* August 1948). All rights reserved. Reprinted by permission of *Commentary* and the author.

Doubleday: Excerpt from *Irrational Man* by William Barrett, copyright © 1958 by William Barrett. Reprinted by permission of Doubleday, a division of Random House, Inc.

Wm. B. Eerdmans Publishing Co.: Excerpt from *Sermons on Job* by John Calvin, translated by Leroy Nixon, copyright © 1952 by Wm. B. Eerdmans Publishing Co. Reprinted by permission of Wm. B. Eerdmans Publishing Co.

The Estate of Archibald MacLeish: Excerpt from "God Has Need of Man" by Archibald MacLeish (Farmington, CT, 1955). Reprinted by permission of The Estate of Archibald MacLeish.

Oxford University Press: Excerpt from *The Idea of the Holy* by Rudolf Otto, translated by John W. Harvey. (Oxford University Press, 2nd edition, 1950). Reprinted by permission of Oxford University Press, Oxford, England.

The University of Chicago Press: Excerpt from *The Religion of Israel* by Yehezkel Kaufmann, translated by Martin Greenberg, copyright © 1960 by The University of Chicago Press. Reprinted by permission of The University of Chicago Press.

CYNTHIA OZICK's essays, novels, and short stories have won numerous prizes and awards, including the American Academy of Arts and Letters Straus Living Award, four O. Henry First Prizes, the Rea Award for the Short Story, and a Guggenheim Fellowship. She lives near New York City.

JOHN F. THORNTON is a literary agent, former book editor, and the coeditor, with Katharine Washburn, of *Dumbing Down* (1996) and *Tongues of Angels, Tongues of Men: A Book of Sermons* (forthcoming, 1999). He lives in New York City.

SUSAN B. VARENNE is a New York City high school teacher with a strong avocational interest in and wide experience of spiritual literature (MA, The University of Chicago Divinity School; Ph.D, Columbia University).

VINTAGE SPIRITUAL CLASSICS

THE CONFESSIONS
by St. Augustine
Translated by Maria Boulding, O.S.B.
Preface by Patricia Hampl
Religion/Spirituality/0-375-70021-8

THE DESERT FATHERS
Translated and Introduced by Helen Waddell
Preface by M. Basil Pennington, O.C.S.O.
Religion/Spirituality/0-375-70019-6

THE IMITATION OF CHRIST
by Thomas à Kempis
Edited and Translated by Joseph N. Tylenda, S.J.
Preface by Sally Cunneen
Religion/Spirituality/0-375-70018-8

THE LITTLE FLOWERS OF ST. FRANCIS OF ASSISI
Edited by and Adapted from a Translation by W. Heywood
Preface by Madeleine L'Engle
Religion/Spirituality/0-375-70020-X

THE RULE OF SAINT BENEDICT
Edited by Timothy Fry, O.S.B.
Preface by Thomas Moore
Religion/Spirituality/0-375-70017-X

Available at your local bookstore, or call toll-free to order:
1-800-793-2665 (credit cards only).